Ukuthwala Bride: A Girl's Escape From Abduction, A Nations New Law

Sibongiseni Masengemu

Published by Sibongiseni Masengemu, 2025.

UKUTHWALA BRIDE: A GIRL'S ESCAPE FROM ABDUCTION, A NATIONS NEW LAW

First edition. August 5, 2025.

ISBN: 979-8231590889

Written by Sibongiseni Masengemu.

Table of Contents

Chapter 1: THE VISIT

Naledi stepped off the bus and stretched her arms, feeling the warm sun on her skin. She hadn't been to her rural relatives in a while, and the familiar sight of the thatched roofs and open fields brought back memories of her childhood. Her aunt, Thembi, was waiting for her with a big smile.

"Naledi, my girl! It's so good to see you!" Thembi exclaimed, enveloping Naledi in a warm hug. Naledi smiled, feeling a mix of excitement and nervousness. She had grown up in the city, and this visit was a chance to reconnect with her roots. But she wasn't sure what to expect. As they walked to the village, Naledi noticed the curious glances from the villagers. She felt a bit self-conscious about her city clothes and hairstyle, but Thembi reassured her with a squeeze on the arm. "We're glad to have you here, Naledi. You'll fit right in," Thembi said.

The path Thembi led her down was a dusty, red-earth trail that wound past maize fields and grazing cattle. Naledi breathed in the scent of wet soil and woodsmoke, a fragrance she associated with the freedom of summer holidays long ago. In the city, the air smelled of exhaust fumes and rain on concrete, a stark contrast to the clean, open space of her aunt's village. She felt a pang of nostalgia, a yearning for the simpler life she remembered.

As they reached Thembi's modest homestead, a young man with a broad, confident smile approached them. "Auntie Thembi, I saw the bus arrive. Is this Naledi?" he asked, his eyes lingering on her. Thembi's face brightened. "Sipho! Yes, this is my brother's daughter. She's come to visit us for a while. Naledi, this is Sipho. He's like a cousin to you—your grandmother and his father were from the same clan." Sipho extended a hand, his grip firm and warm, and Naledi felt a blush creep up her neck.

Sipho didn't seem to mind her city clothes at all. In fact, he seemed intrigued by them. He asked her about the latest fashion, the music, and the fast-paced life of the city. Naledi found herself relaxing in his company, happy to talk about her world. He was handsome, with deep-set eyes and a laugh that seemed to fill the air. She couldn't remember him from her last visit, but she was only a child then, and he must have been a boy. He promised to show her around the village the next day.

The first two days were a blur of new experiences and old memories. Thembi's home was a beehive of activity, with cousins, aunts, and uncles dropping by to greet the city girl. Naledi learned how to pound maize, carry water from the communal tap, and cook on a three-legged pot over an open fire. Her awkward attempts at these tasks were met with good-natured laughter and gentle guidance. Thembi watched her niece with a proud smile, happy to see her getting her hands dirty and embracing her heritage.

Sipho was a constant presence. He was always there, ready to help or to tell a joke. He took her to see the ancient rock paintings on the outskirts of the village, and they sat for hours on a koppie, watching the sunset paint the sky with streaks of orange and purple. He spoke passionately about the traditions of their people, the importance of family, and the way things had always been done. He spoke of the respect for elders and the strength of their community, and Naledi listened, captivated by a world so different from her own.

His words, however, held a certain weight she couldn't quite place. He spoke of the "old ways" and the "proper order of things," and she noticed the other boys her age seemed to hold him in high regard, hanging on his every word. He was clearly a leader, and Naledi felt a strange combination of flattery and unease at his intense focus on her.

She brushed the feeling aside, telling herself it was just the intensity of rural life, so different from the casual indifference of the city.

On the third day, Thembi went to the market in a nearby town, leaving Naledi to look after the younger children. It was a clear, warm afternoon. Sipho arrived, offering to take Naledi on a walk to a hidden waterfall he claimed only the local children knew about. Excited by the prospect of another adventure, Naledi readily agreed. The children were busy with their own games, and the walk would be a welcome break from the day's chores. She pulled on a light jacket and followed him, a feeling of pure trust in her heart.

They walked for a long time, the path growing narrower and the bush thicker. The sounds of the village faded behind them, replaced by the chirping of crickets and the rustling of leaves. The sun was beginning to dip, casting long shadows. Naledi began to feel a little worried. "Sipho, are we almost there? It's getting late," she asked, her voice a little shaky. Sipho's smile was still there, but it seemed different now, a little too fixed. "Don't worry, Naledi. We're almost there. Just a little further," he said, taking her hand. His grip was tight, not friendly anymore.

Her fear spiked when they crested a small hill and she saw not a waterfall, but a group of men waiting. They were all older than Sipho and looked serious, their faces grim in the fading light. They stood in a circle, and in the middle, a fire was already beginning to crackle. Naledi pulled her hand away, her heart pounding. "Sipho, what is this?" she demanded, her voice a whisper of panic. He didn't answer, but simply nodded to the men. They started chanting, a low, rhythmic sound that sent a shiver down her spine.

Sipho stepped forward and placed a hand on her shoulder. "Don't be scared, Naledi. This is what we talked about. This is tradition. This is the way of our people." He gestured to the men, who had now started dancing around the fire. "It's called *ukuthwala*. It is our culture. I am claiming you as my bride." He said the words with a sense of ceremony, as if this was the most natural thing in the world. He expected her to understand, to simply accept.

Naledi's mind reeled. *Ukuthwala?* Bride? She was only fifteen years old. She was not a bride. This was not a proposal; this was an abduction. Panic gave way to a cold, hard resolve. She had to get away. She tried to run, but two of the men grabbed her arms, holding her fast. She screamed, but her voice was swallowed by the vast, open space and the rhythmic chanting of the men. It was a terrifying, isolating moment.

Back in the village, Thembi returned from the market to an empty house. The younger children told her Naledi had gone with Sipho to see a waterfall. Thembi, with a sinking feeling, immediately knew something was wrong. She went to Sipho's family homestead, but was met with cold shoulders. His father, an elder in the community, informed her that Naledi was now Sipho's bride and that it was an old custom. Thembi's heart broke, the very customs she had spoken of with pride now used as a weapon against her own niece.

Thembi and her husband refused to accept this. They did not believe in a tradition that took a child without her or her family's consent. They knew this was not a matter of culture, but a crime. Ignoring the scoffs and warnings of the villagers, Thembi called Naledi's parents in the city. The phone call was filled with Thembi's tearful explanations and Naledi's father's enraged, disbelieving questions. By morning, Naledi's family had opened a case with the police, setting in motion a chain of events that would pit tradition against the law and family against family.

CHAPTER 2: A PARENTS FURY

The phone call came in the dead of the night, a harsh, invasive ring that shattered the quiet peace of Thabo and Lerato's city apartment. Thabo, a man of routine and order, was already in bed. He grumbled, fumbling for his phone, expecting a work emergency. The voice on the other end was Thembi's, but it was not the cheerful, familiar tone he knew. It was ragged with fear and tears, and the words she spoke made his blood run cold.

"It's Naledi," she sobbed. "Sipho took her. He says it's *ukuthwala*." Thabo's mind, still thick with sleep, struggled to process the information. The name *ukuthwala* was a dusty echo from his own rural childhood, a custom he thought had long since faded. But Thembi's words left no room for doubt. "He's claiming her as his bride, Thabo. Our daughter. She's only fifteen." He dropped the phone, his face a mask of disbelief and fury.

Lerato, jolted awake by the crash of the phone and the look on her husband's face, sat bolt upright in bed. "Thabo, what is it? What happened?" she asked, her voice laced with dread. He scooped the phone back up and put it on speaker, his hand shaking. As Thembi repeated the story, Lerato's face went white. The image of their bright, vibrant daughter, now a victim of a cruel, outdated practice, was a physical blow. Their beautiful, happy home suddenly felt like a cage, and the city, a million miles away from where their child was held.

They were at the police station within the hour, their clothes mismatched and their faces haggard. The air in the station was stale and cold, filled with the hum of fluorescent lights and the distant murmur of voices. They were met by a young officer who listened with a skeptical expression. "Ma'am, sir, you're saying your daughter was taken for a custom? This sounds like a family matter, not a police one." His dismissive tone was a fresh wave of agony.

Thabo slammed his hand on the counter. "This is not a family matter! It is a crime! My daughter is a child, and she has been kidnapped! Is that not a crime?" His voice echoed in the cavernous room, attracting the attention of other officers. The young officer, taken aback by the fury in Thabo's eyes, changed his tone. He took down their information, but the reluctance in his movements spoke volumes.

"We will contact the authorities in that area, sir," he said, handing them a case number. "We will do our best." His words felt hollow, a bureaucratic formality. They left the station feeling more helpless than when they had arrived, armed with nothing but a flimsy piece of paper and a promise that felt as fragile as glass. The city, which had always felt like a beacon of modernity and justice, now felt indifferent and slow.

The rest of the night was an endless torment. They sat in their living room, the silence between them heavy with unspeakable fear. Every creak of the floorboards, every distant siren, seemed to mock their powerlessness. Lerato clutched a photo of Naledi from her last birthday, her daughter's joyful face smiling up at her. "She was so excited to go," Lerato whispered, her voice cracking. "She wanted to see where you grew up, Thabo."

Thabo looked at the photo, his jaw tight. He thought of his own youth, of the traditions he had left behind, believing they were relics of the past. He never imagined they could reach out and snatch his daughter. He felt a deep, wrenching guilt. He should have known. He should have warned her. He should have stayed connected. He had let his daughter walk into a world he no longer understood, and now she was paying the price.

The sun rose on a grey, muted city, casting weak light into their empty home. Lerato made them tea, but the cups remained untouched.

Every time the phone rang, their hearts leaped into their throats, only to sink again with each wrong number. The waiting was a slow form of torture, a silence more painful than any sound. It was the longest morning of their lives, each minute stretching into an eternity.

When the call finally came, it was from the police in the city. The news was exactly what they had feared. The rural authorities were facing resistance from the villagers. Sipho's father was an elder, a man of influence, and he had claimed the abduction was a matter of custom. The local police were caught in the middle, hesitant to act against a powerful community figure, and unwilling to escalate the situation.

Thabo's anger, which had been a simmering, low flame all night, now erupted into a cold, focused fire. He stood up, pacing the room with a determined stride. "We can't wait for them," he said, his voice hard. "They will do nothing. This is our daughter. This is on us now." He looked at Lerato, his eyes pleading for her to understand. "We have to go. We have to go there and bring her home ourselves."

Lerato didn't hesitate. The thought of confronting the same family that had betrayed her daughter's trust filled her with a righteous fury. She knew it would be a difficult and dangerous journey, a confrontation that would tear apart the fragile bridge between her family and Thabo's. But a mother's love knows no fear. "Let's go," she said, her voice quiet but firm. "Let's go get our girl."

They packed a single bag, not with holiday clothes, but with essentials for a long, difficult fight. Lerato put Naledi's picture carefully into her handbag, a small, paper amulet to remind her of what she was fighting for. Thabo grabbed his car keys, his knuckles white with tension. The silence of the house was now filled with the hurried rustle of their movements, a renewed sense of purpose replacing the paralyzing fear.

As they drove out of the city, the concrete towers giving way to the sprawling outskirts, Thabo's mind was a maelstrom of thoughts. He wondered what Naledi was doing. Was she scared? Was she hurt? Was she waiting for them? He imagined her terrified face, and the thought was a searing brand on his soul. He had to be strong for Lerato, but inside, he was a father in an abyss of pain.

Lerato stared out the window, watching the landscape change from the familiar grey of the urban landscape to the verdant hills of the countryside. She was going into a world she didn't know, a world that was now holding her daughter hostage. She thought of her daughter's dreams, of the bright future Naledi had planned for herself, a future she now feared had been stolen. She would not let that happen. She would fight.

The sun was high in the sky when they finally arrived at the village, the air thick with the smell of woodsmoke and dust, the same fragrance Naledi had inhaled with a sense of wonder just days before. They drove past Thembi's homestead, their eyes fixed on the path that led deeper into the community. The village felt different now, not a place of nostalgia, but a battlefield. They were here, and they were ready to fight for their child.

CHAPTER 3: GATHERING OF ELDERS

The village, which Naledi had seen as a place of rustic charm, now appeared to Thabo and Lerato as a wall of silent opposition. They drove to Thembi's homestead, where their car was met with a mixture of relief and trepidation. Thembi rushed out to meet them, her face a road map of worry. "Oh, Thabo, Lerato, I am so glad you are here," she said, her voice a low, urgent whisper. "It is not good. They will not listen."

Thabo's jaw was set. "We are not here to listen. We are here to get our daughter." Thembi led them into her hut, a small, dark space that felt safe from the judging eyes of the village. She explained the situation in more detail: Sipho's father, Mkhulu, an elder of significant standing, was refusing to acknowledge the police report. He insisted the matter was a cultural rite, a marriage, and that the city law had no place in their traditions. The local police, caught between a powerful elder and the angry city family, were hesitant to act.

Lerato, still clutching Naledi's photo, spoke for the first time since they had left the city. "Where is she, Thembi? Where have they taken her?" Thembi's eyes filled with tears. "I do not know for sure. Mkhulu says she is safe, that she is with his sister, learning the ways of a new wife. But Thabo, a girl is not a bride at fifteen. This is not the way." She shook her head, a deep shame etched on her face. "This is not the *ukuthwala* of our people. This is a perversion."

After a tense, brief discussion, Thembi's husband, a quiet man named Jabulani, came forward. "The elders have been called to gather.

They will see you. This is your chance to speak to them." The meeting was not an offer, but a summons. It was the village's way of asserting their authority, their way of controlling the narrative. Thabo and Lerato knew they had no choice but to go. This was their only path to Naledi.

The gathering took place under the spreading branches of a giant acacia tree. A dozen or so men and women sat on wooden stools, their faces impassive. In the center, on a carved chair, sat Mkhulu, Sipho's father. He was a large man with a powerful presence, his eyes hard and unyielding as they fell upon Thabo. He saw not a father in distress, but a city man who had forgotten his roots, a man who had brought a foreign law to their sacred customs.

Thabo, who had prepared a forceful speech, felt his carefully constructed words crumble under the weight of their collective gaze. He began to speak, his voice wavering slightly. He spoke of his love for his daughter, of her dreams, of the law of the country. He spoke of the difference between a respectful tradition and a criminal act. He spoke as a father, a man who had lost his child. But his words seemed to fall on deaf ears, bouncing off the silent wall of their disapproval.

When he finished, Mkhulu spoke, his voice deep and slow. "You speak of a child. We see a woman of fifteen, a fertile field ready for planting. You speak of the city's law, a law that has forgotten the ways of our ancestors. Our custom, *ukuthwala*, is not a crime. It is a time-honored tradition that ensures our lineage, that strengthens our community." He looked at Lerato with thinly veiled contempt. "Your daughter is with her new family. She is where she is meant to be. We have spoken. The matter is closed."

A low murmur of agreement rippled through the gathered elders. The meeting was over. They were dismissed. As they walked away, Lerato could feel the weight of their collective disapproval, the icy disdain that settled over them like a shroud. They had come here seeking justice and found a tribunal. They had come to rescue their daughter and found that the community itself was her captor.

Back at Thembi's homestead, the full reality of their situation settled over them like a heavy, suffocating blanket. The police had been called, but they were hesitant. The elders had heard their pleas, but had dismissed them entirely. They were strangers in their own land, outsiders in a battle against deeply entrenched traditions and a man who wielded more power than any city official could. Thabo ran his hand through his hair, his face a mask of defeat. "What do we do now, Lerato? What can we do?"

Lerato's fury, which had been simmering beneath a calm exterior, now hardened into an unshakeable resolve. She looked at Thabo, her eyes blazing with a fierce, maternal fire. "We find her ourselves," she said, her voice quiet but firm. "We came here to get our daughter, and we will not leave without her. If the law and the elders will not help us, then we will do this alone. We will not fail her."

CHAPTER 4: THE PERSUIT

Lerato's words hung in the air, a final, unyielding challenge to the indifference of the world around them. Thabo looked at his wife, seeing in her eyes a strength he hadn't known she possessed. "You're right," he said, his voice now calm and decisive. "We'll do it ourselves." Thembi, who had been listening in silent despair, looked up, her face a mix of fear and admiration. "You can't go alone," she said. "I may not agree with what Sipho has done, but this is a dangerous place for a city man and woman to go looking for trouble. Jabulani and I will help. We know the land."

The plan was simple, born of Thembi's intimate knowledge of the village. She knew that in cases of *ukuthwala*, the girl was often taken to a relative's homestead to be 'prepared' for her new life, away from the immediate drama of the family. The most likely place, she told them in a hushed voice, was the home of Mkhulu's sister, a woman known as MaZondo, who lived in a small, isolated cluster of huts on the other side of the river. The place was difficult to reach and even harder to find, a deliberate choice meant to thwart any who might try to intervene.

As the sun began to set, casting a deep orange glow over the hills, Thabo, Lerato, and Jabulani set out. Thembi stayed behind to keep watch and to give them an alibi should anyone ask questions. The journey was treacherous. The path was little more than a goat trail, winding through dense thorn bushes and over rocky terrain. Jabulani, a silent guide, led the way with a small torch, his familiar strides making the impossible ground seem navigable. Thabo and Lerato, however, stumbled and scraped their way along, their city shoes ill-suited for the rugged path.

The air grew cool and thick with the nocturnal sounds of the African bush. The distant howl of a jackal, the rustle of a snake in the dry grass, and the omnipresent hum of crickets created a symphony of unease. Thabo's mind raced with fear, his heart pounding not just from the exertion but from the chilling thought of what he would find. Would Naledi be safe? Would she even want to come with them? Would he have to fight for her?

Meanwhile, in MaZondo's compound, Naledi sat huddled in a small, dark hut. She was no longer wearing her city clothes. MaZondo, a stern-faced woman with an aura of unshakable authority, had given her a traditional wrapper and told her to put on her doek, a headscarf. Her phone, her last connection to the world she knew, had been taken from her. The days had been a blur of forced lessons in how to be a 'proper wife,' how to cook a meal for a man, how to be silent and respectful.

Naledi's heart was a hollow ache of loneliness and terror. She thought of her parents, of her life back in the city, of the friends she had been laughing with just a week ago. She didn't understand this tradition. She didn't want it. Every time MaZondo tried to teach her, Naledi met her with a stone-faced silence, her defiance the only small piece of her identity she had left. She refused to learn, she refused to cooperate. This was not her life, and she would not accept it.

MaZondo, for her part, was not cruel. She was a woman of deep faith in the old ways, and she saw Naledi's rebellion not as a girl's panic, but as the misplaced arrogance of a city child. She would break her, she was sure of it. All girls, no matter how headstrong, eventually learned their place. It was for their own good. She had heard stories of girls who had run away, of girls who had fought, and they always came back, humbled and grateful.

As night fell, a low, flickering fire cast dancing shadows on the walls of Naledi's hut. She sat on the dirt floor, her legs tucked beneath her, her mind replaying the horror of that first night. Sipho had come to see her, his smile still broad, still confident. He spoke to her of their future, of the children they would have, of his love for her. But Naledi saw only a monster. She would not speak to him. She would not even look at him.

Sipho, however, was undeterred. He was a hunter who had claimed his prize, and he knew he would have to be patient. His father had told him to wait, to let her learn, to let her see the truth of their way of life. She was a city girl, wild and untamed, but she would come around. He was sure of it. He left her with a final, chilling promise: "You will be my wife, Naledi. You will see that this is your destiny."

Back on the river bank, Jabulani led them to a narrow, rocky crossing. The water was dark and swift, and the air was cold. They waded through the current, the water up to their knees, and emerged shivering on the other side. The climb to MaZondo's homestead was steep, their tired legs burning with effort. Finally, they reached the top of the hill, and below them, they could see a cluster of four huts, their windows glowing with the soft light of oil lamps.

They moved stealthily, creeping through the shadows of the compound. Jabulani pointed to a hut slightly separated from the others. "That is likely the one. MaZondo would want to keep her away from the rest of the household." Thabo and Lerato crept towards the hut, their hearts in their throats. They peeked through a small gap in the mud wall, and what they saw made their world stop. Naledi, their daughter, sat on the floor, her back to them. But across from her, sitting by the flickering firelight, were MaZondo, and Sipho. The confrontation was upon them.

CHAPTER 5: THE CONFRONTATION

The sight of their daughter, dressed in strange clothes and sitting in a dark hut, was a physical blow. Thabo felt a primal roar build in his chest, a sound that was a mix of a father's rage and a man's despair. He didn't think; he simply acted. Pushing the flimsy wooden door aside, he burst into the hut, Lerato right behind him. The sudden rush of cold night air and the sight of their furious faces extinguished the small, flickering fire of the oil lamp.

Naledi's head snapped up. Her eyes, wide with shock, met her father's, and the dam of her defiance broke. "Papa!" she cried, a choked sob escaping her lips. She scrambled to her feet, her legs unsteady, and ran into her mother's arms. Lerato enveloped her, holding her so tightly she could feel the frantic pounding of her daughter's heart. She buried her face in Naledi's hair, breathing in the scent of smoke and fear, and wept with a mixture of relief and unbridled fury.

The chaos of the parents' arrival had stunned MaZondo and Sipho into silence for a moment. But the quiet was short-lived. Sipho, his confident smile gone, rose to his feet. "What is this?" he demanded, his voice low and hostile. "Who told you where to come? This is a private matter. She is my wife now. You have no right to be here." He took a menacing step towards them, but Jabulani, who had entered the hut behind Thabo, stepped in front of him, his body a silent barrier.

"Sipho, you will not speak to her like that," Jabulani said, his voice quiet but firm. "And you will not call her your wife. She is a child, and this is an abomination. Thembi and I will not stand for it." Sipho looked at Jabulani, his eyes filled with disbelief. It was a clear act of betrayal, a family member siding with the outsiders. The tension in the small hut was a palpable, living thing.

Thabo's fury, which had momentarily been drowned out by his relief, returned in full force. He stepped away from Lerato and Naledi, his fists clenched at his sides. "Don't you dare speak of her as if she is yours!" he spat, his voice trembling with anger. "You are a criminal! You kidnapped my daughter! The police have been notified. You will be arrested for this!" His words, spoken in the language of the city, seemed to bounce off Sipho, who simply sneered.

"The police? What are they going to do? This is our land. This is our tradition," Sipho said, gesturing to MaZondo, who now stood with her arms crossed, a look of profound disapproval on her face. "You left this world, Thabo. You took your city ways and you left us behind. But we do not forget our culture. Your daughter is a woman now. She has been claimed, and a bride price has been paid to the community. The matter is done."

Lerato, still holding Naledi, looked at MaZondo with a gaze so fierce it could have melted stone. "You are a mother, are you not? How could you do this to another mother's child? To take her and force her into something she does not want, under the guise of tradition? This is not culture. This is a sickness." Her words were like venom, cutting through the thin veil of MaZondo's self-righteousness.

MaZondo, for the first time, seemed to waver. She looked at Naledi, huddled in her mother's arms, her body shaking with silent sobs. The girl was clearly terrified, a far cry from the sullen, defiant child MaZondo had been trying to 'teach.' Still, she composed herself, her face hardening. "The girl does not know what is good for her," she said, her voice strained. "We are simply showing her the way. You have confused her with your city talk of freedom and independence. You have made her soft."

The argument escalated, their voices rising and clashing in the small space. Thabo spoke of Naledi's legal rights, of the constitutional protection against child marriage. Sipho spoke of the authority of the elders, of the sacredness of the *ukuthwala* custom. Lerato spoke of a mother's heart, of the right of every girl to choose her own path. Jabulani, a man of few words, spoke of the community, of how Mkhulu's actions had shamed them all.

Suddenly, a loud, authoritative voice boomed from the doorway. "Enough!" Mkhulu, Sipho's father, stood framed in the opening, a formidable silhouette against the night sky. He was not alone. Behind him stood several other village elders, their faces grim and serious. "What is all this shouting? This is not the way of our people. There is a proper time and place for matters of this importance."

Mkhulu stepped into the hut, his gaze sweeping over the scene—Naledi clinging to her parents, Jabulani standing guard, and Sipho glowering with a mixture of anger and humiliation. He turned his gaze on Thabo, his eyes a cold fire. "You have broken the rules of hospitality, Thabo. You have come here like a thief in the night, disrupting a sacred ceremony. You have brought the poison of the city to our home. You will not take this girl tonight. She is under my protection now."

The statement was a command, a final word from a man who expected no debate. Thabo's heart sank. He looked at the faces of the elders behind Mkhulu and saw only unwavering support for their leader. They had walked into a trap. They had found their daughter, but they were still powerless to take her. They were surrounded, outnumbered, and outmaneuvered.

Lerato, however, would not be silenced. "We will not leave without her," she said, her voice shaking with emotion. "She is coming home with us, tonight, or we will bring the police to every doorstep in this village. You cannot keep our child." The threat, while defiant, was also a desperate plea, a last resort in a battle of wills she knew they were losing.

Mkhulu's expression didn't change. He simply nodded to two of the elders, who stepped forward and gently but firmly separated Naledi from her parents. "The matter is not over, city man," Mkhulu said, a chilling smile on his lips. "It is just beginning. You may go now. We will discuss this with you, and the police, in the morning. For now, your daughter will remain here, with her new family, where she belongs."

CHAPTER 6: A LONG NIGHT OF WAITING

The walk back to Thembi's homestead was a silent, agonizing mirror of the journey they had just made. Before, their steps had been fueled by a desperate hope; now, they were heavy with the weight of defeat. Naledi's face, etched with terror as she was pulled from her mother's arms, was a searing image in Lerato's mind. Thabo, walking ahead, was a statue of contained rage, his fists still clenched, his breath coming in short, sharp bursts. Jabulani, their quiet guide, had nothing to say. The three of them walked in a cloud of shared failure.

They found Thembi huddled by the fire, waiting. The moment she saw their empty hands and defeated expressions, her face crumpled. "Oh, my sister," she said to Lerato, her voice a whisper of pure sympathy. "I am so sorry. I knew Mkhulu would do this. His pride is a hard and unforgiving thing." She held Lerato close, rocking her gently as the dam of Lerato's composure finally broke. The silent sobs turned into a loud, heart-wrenching cry, a mother's wail for her stolen child.

Thabo could not bear to be in the hut. He walked outside, pacing the homestead's yard under the indifferent gaze of a star-filled sky. He felt a deep, wrenching guilt. He had left this world to seek a better life, a life where his daughter would be free. He had told himself he was a modern man, and that the old traditions were a thing of the past. Now, those very traditions had reached out and taken the one person he was meant to protect. His failure was not just a personal one; it was a failure of his entire life's philosophy.

Inside the compound, Naledi was once again alone. After her parents were forced to leave, MaZondo had looked at her with a new, chilling determination. "You see?" she had said. "They have come, and they have gone. Your city talk and your city law mean nothing here. They will come back in the morning and we will deal with this. Until then, you will sit. You will think. You will realize that you are our family now." Sipho had said nothing, his face a mask of silent triumph.

Naledi's mind, which had been a whirlwind of panic, now settled into a cold, fierce resolve. Seeing her parents, feeling her mother's arms around her, had reminded her of who she was. She was not a 'bride.' She was Naledi. She was a daughter, a student, a girl with dreams. She would not sit and accept this. She would not be broken. She would wait, she would watch, and she would find a way out. Her small act of defiance—sitting with her back to the door, not touching the food they had offered her—was all she had left.

The long night stretched on, a chasm of fear and separation. In Thembi's hut, Thabo and Lerato sat in a numb silence, their eyes fixed on the entrance, as if Naledi would appear at any moment. They talked through the plan for the morning: they would call the police again, this time with a formal statement of kidnapping and child endangerment. They would demand that the law be upheld, no matter the local traditions. They would not back down, not this time.

Lerato, in a rare moment of stillness, laid a hand on Thabo's arm. "We will get her back," she whispered, her voice still raw from crying. "We will not leave without her." Thabo looked at her, his face grim. "I know," he said. "I should have fought him, Lerato. I should have... " She shook her head. "No. You did what you had to do. We are in their world now. We must play by their rules, and their rules are not ours. The real fight begins in the light of day. When the law, and the city, finally comes to this place."

Meanwhile, back in his hut, Sipho sat with his father, Mkhulu. He was glowing with pride. "See, Father? The girl's parents came, and they were like flies buzzing around a lion. They could do nothing." Mkhulu, however, was a man of more caution. "Do not be so quick to celebrate, my son. The city law is like a snake in the tall grass. You do not see it until it strikes. You have stirred up a great storm. The whole village will be watching. The elders are with us, but they can be swayed. You must be prepared."

Mkhulu's warning did little to temper Sipho's celebratory mood. He had claimed his bride. He had stood up to the city man who had forgotten his heritage. He was a man of the village, and he had won. The community, he thought, would rally around him. He felt a profound sense of destiny, a feeling that he was not just taking a bride, but upholding a sacred way of life. He was a hero in his own story, a defender of tradition against the insidious corruption of the outside world.

The long night finally gave way to a sliver of grey light on the horizon. A new day had arrived. In Thembi's compound, Thabo and Lerato rose, their eyes red from lack of sleep, but their resolve stronger than ever. They were no longer just a father and mother. They were a force of nature, a hurricane of parental fury that had finally found its direction. They had come to this village as visitors, but they would leave as warriors, fighting for their daughter's freedom against an entire community that had turned against them.

CHAPTER 7: THE BREAK OF DAY

The new day dawned not with the soft light of a new beginning, but with a harsh, unforgiving grey that mirrored the mood of Thembi's homestead. The air was thick with the scent of woodsmoke and the quiet menace of a looming battle. Thabo and Lerato, their faces pale and drawn, were already up. They had no time for breakfast or pleasantries. Their mission was clear, their path set: they would go to the local police station and make sure their report was heard, and this time, acted upon.

They drove to the small, dusty police station in a nearby town, a place that felt more like a forgotten outpost than a bastion of justice. The same officer from the night before was there, his expression now a mixture of weariness and concern. "We have contacted the station here," Thabo said, his voice hard. "We are here to file a formal report of kidnapping. My daughter, Naledi, is a minor, and she is being held against her will. We know where she is. We need you to come with us, now."

The officer sighed, running a hand through his short hair. "Sir, I have been talking to the elders. They say this is a traditional matter. The girl is under the protection of her future husband's family. There are no charges. We cannot simply go in and seize her." His words were a direct echo of Mkhulu's, a clear indication that the influence of the elder stretched far beyond the village borders. Lerato stepped forward, her quiet rage a potent weapon.

"Do you have a daughter?" she asked, her voice low and dangerous. "A child? Would you stand by and let her be taken from you, for some 'tradition' you do not believe in? This is not culture; it is an abduction. And if you do not do your duty and enforce the law, then we will go to the highest court in this land. We will find a way, and when we do, we will make sure that every official who stood by and did nothing will be held accountable. This is a promise."

The threat, delivered with a mother's fierce conviction, hit its mark. The officer looked at the raw emotion in Lerato's eyes and finally understood that this was not a simple family dispute. This was a battle for a child's life and freedom. He nodded slowly. "We will come with you," he said, his voice now filled with a new, hesitant sense of purpose. "But we must be careful. We must do this by the book. These are powerful people, and they will fight us every step of the way."

Meanwhile, in MaZondo's compound, Naledi was a flurry of silent activity. The long night of sitting had done nothing to break her spirit; in fact, it had hardened it into a cold, unbreakable resolve. She was hungry, thirsty, and terrified, but a small, defiant flame burned in her heart. She was a city girl. She knew how to think fast. She knew how to survive. MaZondo was in the main hut, preparing for the day's meeting, leaving Naledi unguarded for the first time since she had arrived.

Naledi's phone, her last lifeline, was her first priority. She had seen MaZondo put it on a high shelf in the main hut, a symbolic act of severing her from her old life. She crept out of her own hut, her bare feet silent on the dusty ground. She was a ghost in her own prison, a child who had been forced to become a phantom. The compound was quiet, the younger children not yet awake, the men already out in the fields. The air was cool, the sun just beginning to peek over the horizon.

She reached the main hut and slid silently through the doorway, her eyes darting around the small space. MaZondo's back was to her, as she stirred a large pot over the open fire, a slow, rhythmic movement that filled the room with the scent of maize porridge. Naledi's heart pounded, a frantic drum against her ribs. She saw the shelf. Her phone was there, a small, black rectangle that represented everything she had lost.

With the quiet grace of a cat, she moved. She reached up, her fingers just brushing the edge of the phone. But in her haste, she knocked a small, carved wooden cup from the shelf. It clattered to the floor, the sound shattering the morning silence like a gunshot. MaZondo's head snapped up. Her eyes, filled with a sudden, chilling suspicion, locked onto Naledi.

The girl froze, her hand still reaching for the phone, the world slowing to a halt. The cup lay on the floor between them, a silent accuser. MaZondo's face, which had been impassive, now broke into a grim, knowing smile. She said nothing, but her eyes, cold and hard, told Naledi all she needed to know. The window of escape had just slammed shut.

CHAPTER 8: THE LAW ARRIVES

The silence that followed the cup's clatter was more terrifying than any sound. Naledi, frozen in place, watched as MaZondo's grim smile widened into something cold and knowing. The older woman didn't shout or reprimand her. She simply walked over, her movements deliberate and heavy, and picked up the small wooden cup. Her eyes, however, never left Naledi's face. "The things you are trying to hold onto from your old life will only lead you astray," she said, her voice a low murmur. She then walked to the shelf, took Naledi's phone, and without a word, walked out of the hut. The door closed behind her, leaving Naledi in a newfound, chilling solitude, with no hope of contact.

Meanwhile, Thabo and Lerato were in the back of the small police van, its tires kicking up a cloud of red dust. The officer, Sergeant Dube, drove with a tense focus, his knuckles white on the steering wheel. He had called for backup, two more officers who were now following in a separate vehicle, a clear indication that he anticipated trouble. "They will not like this," he said, more to himself than to them. "Mkhulu is a man of great respect here. We are going against the entire community."

Lerato, her hand in Thabo's, looked out the window at the familiar landscape that now felt so alien. The rolling hills, the scattered homesteads—it all seemed to conspire against them. She was no longer just a mother looking for her child; she was a city woman, an outsider, a symbol of a world the villagers had clearly rejected. She could only pray that the sight of the police would be enough to break the hold of tradition and fear.

The police van's arrival at MaZondo's compound was met with a stunned silence. The women and children, who had been going about their morning chores, stopped and stared. The sight of the official vehicle was a jarring intrusion, a sign that the outside world had finally found its way to their doorstep. Mkhulu, along with a few other elders and Sipho, emerged from the main hut, their faces a mixture of defiance and quiet authority.

Sergeant Dube stepped out of the van, his uniform crisp and his expression serious. "We are here for the girl, Naledi," he announced, his voice carrying in the sudden quiet. "She is a minor, and she is being held against her will. This is a matter of law, not tradition." Mkhulu stepped forward, his massive frame a wall of opposition. "Sergeant," he said, his voice slow and deliberate. "You are a man of our people. You know that this is not a matter for the law. This is a family matter. The girl is here of her own free will. She is our daughter now."

The standoff was tense, the air thick with unspoken threats. Thabo, stepping out of the van, felt a renewed surge of anger. "She is not your daughter!" he shouted, his voice cracking with emotion. "She is my daughter! And you have no right to hold her here!" Sipho, standing behind his father, met Thabo's gaze with a cold, triumphant smile. He saw the city man as a defeated enemy, a ghost from a past he was determined to erase.

Sergeant Dube, seeing that the situation was escalating, held up a hand. "Let us not argue in the street. Let us do this in a civilized way. We will speak to the girl. We will hear her side of the story. If she wants to go with her parents, then she will go. If she wishes to stay, then we must follow her wishes." He was trying to find a middle ground, a way to de-escalate the situation without compromising his duty. But both sides knew that in this moment, there could be no middle ground.

Naledi, who had been sitting in her hut, heard the commotion and felt a renewed surge of hope. She crept to the door, peeking out through a crack. She saw the police van, the officers in their uniforms, and her parents. Her heart pounded with a desperate mix of relief and fear. The confrontation was happening. This was her chance. She just had to find the courage to speak.

MaZondo, seeing her peeking, grabbed Naledi's arm and pulled her into the yard. "Here she is," she said, her voice dripping with contempt. "Let her speak for herself. Let her tell you all what she wants." Naledi was pushed into the center of the yard, a small, terrified figure caught between two worlds. On one side stood her parents, their faces a roadmap of their love and fear. On the other stood Mkhulu and Sipho, their faces hard and unyielding.

Sergeant Dube knelt down, trying to meet her eyes. "Naledi," he said softly, "your parents have come for you. They say you are being held here against your will. We are here to help you. Do you want to go home with them? Or do you wish to stay here?" The question hung in the air, a question that was meant to be simple, but was now a life-altering choice. Naledi looked at her parents, then at Sipho, then at the silent, watching faces of the villagers. This was her moment. This was the one chance she had to speak her truth.

CHAPTER 9: NALEDI'S CHOICE

The question from Sergeant Dube hung in the air, a final, definitive choice that Naledi felt had the power to sever her very soul in two. The world around her had narrowed to a single, focused point of tension. On one side, her parents stood, their love and fear a tangible, almost physical force reaching out to her. Their faces were a mirror of her own pain, their eyes pleading with her to make the right choice, the safe choice. On the other side, Mkhulu and Sipho watched her, their expressions hard and unyielding. They represented a different world, a different kind of pressure—the weight of tradition, of community expectation, of a path that had been carved for her without her consent.

Her gaze fell on Sipho, the boy who had shown her the beauty of the landscape and the promise of a friendship, only to betray her in the most profound way. He stood with his arms crossed, a flicker of confident triumph in his eyes, as if her answer was a foregone conclusion. She could see his story already written: a young man who had successfully claimed his city bride, a hero who had upheld the customs of his people. That image, the pride and the ownership in his stare, was a cold shock to her system. She was not a prize to be won. She was not a part of his story. She was the author of her own.

A small memory, sharp and clear, cut through the fog of her fear. She remembered sitting on the koppie with Sipho, watching the sunset, listening to him talk about the "old ways." She had been so captivated by his words, so eager to understand this new world. But she realized now that his words had not been an offering of knowledge; they had been a warning, a prelude to his plan. She remembered the feeling of her phone being taken, her voice being silenced, her identity being erased. This was not the freedom she had craved. This was a prison built of tradition.

She looked at the ground, at the red, dusty earth that had been so welcoming just a week ago and now felt like the soil of a foreign land. She took a deep breath, and when she raised her head, her eyes were no longer filled with fear. They were filled with a fierce, quiet resolve. She looked at Sergeant Dube, and then directly at Mkhulu, her voice shaky at first, but gaining strength with every word. "I want to go home," she said. "I want to go with my parents."

The words, so simple and yet so powerful, hung in the silence. The collective gasp of the women in the compound was the only sound. Mkhulu's face, which had been so sure and confident, now looked as if it had been carved from stone. Sipho's triumphant smile faltered, replaced by a look of shock and disbelief. He had been so certain of his victory, so convinced that she would choose his world over her own.

Lerato let out a sob of relief, and Thabo rushed forward, wrapping her in a tight hug. Naledi clung to her father, feeling the warmth and safety of his embrace, a physical reminder of everything she had almost lost. Sergeant Dube, his face a mixture of relief and professionalism, stepped forward. "The matter is settled," he said, his voice loud and clear. "The girl has made her choice. She is to go with her parents. This is the law."

Mkhulu, however, was not so easily defeated. "This is not over," he said, his voice a low growl. "You have broken our tradition. You have disrespected our customs. The bride price has been paid. There will be consequences." His words were a threat, a final attempt to assert his authority. But in the face of Naledi's choice and the presence of the law, they were powerless.

Thabo and Lerato, with Naledi walking between them, her hand firmly in both of theirs, walked to the police van. The other officers stood at attention, a silent, official barrier between the family and the sullen, defeated faces of the villagers. As they got into the van, Naledi looked back one last time. The village, once a place of childhood memories, now felt like a ghost, a place she had visited and escaped, leaving a part of her innocence behind.

The van drove away, leaving a cloud of red dust in its wake. In the back, Naledi sat huddled between her parents, the silence broken only by the quiet hum of the vehicle. She was safe, she was free. But she knew in her heart that this was not the end. It was only the beginning of a different kind of journey, one that would involve not just healing, but a long, difficult fight for justice.

CHAPTER 10: LONG ROAD HOME

The drive away from the village was a slow, deliberate procession. The police van, a jarring symbol of an alien authority, kicked up a trail of red dust that seemed to obscure the memories of the last few days. In the back, Naledi was wedged between her parents, her small body shaking with exhaustion and a delayed, quiet terror. She was home, in her parents' arms, but the feeling of safety was a fragile thing, a delicate shell that could be shattered by the slightest memory. Her mother's hand was a warm, firm presence on her knee, a constant anchor against the emotional current that threatened to pull her under.

Thabo, sitting on her other side, was a silent pillar of strength. His face was a mask of grim determination, his anger a quiet hum beneath the surface. He had lost his temper, he had pleaded, but in the end, it was his daughter's strength that had saved them all. He was immensely proud of her, but his pride was tempered by a deep, wrenching guilt. He should have known. He should have protected her. He had brought her to this place, and she had been forced to face a darkness he had left behind long ago.

As they drove, Naledi felt the physical landscape shift around her. The dusty, thorn-bush-filled roads gave way to paved highways, the scattered homesteads to rows of small houses, and finally, to the sprawling, vibrant chaos of the city. The noise, which had once been the soundtrack of her life, now felt like a jarring symphony. The smell of exhaust fumes and street food, once a comforting scent, now felt overwhelming. She was back in her world, but she felt like a stranger, an interloper who had just returned from a brutal war.

The first few days back were a blur of police interviews, doctors' visits, and long, quiet conversations with her parents. Lerato was a force of nature, a calm and steady presence who refused to let Naledi sink into her trauma. She cooked Naledi's favorite meals, she sat with her for hours, she held her hand and listened without judgment as Naledi, in fits and starts, told her story. The story of Sipho's easy charm, of the unsettling feel of the *ukuthwala* ceremony, of the horrifying moment she realized she was not a bride, but a captive.

Thabo, for his part, was consumed by a righteous fury. He was a man of the city, a man who believed in the power of the law. He had promised Mkhulu there would be consequences, and he was determined to see that promise through. He spent hours on the phone with his lawyer, a sharp, no-nonsense woman named Ms. Maseko, who listened to his story with a combination of professional detachment and quiet outrage. "This is a serious crime, Thabo," she said. "We will not let this stand."

Sipho and Mkhulu, however, were not sitting idly by. News of the incident had spread through the village like wildfire. The community was split. Some saw Sipho as a hero, a young man who had bravely upheld tradition against the meddling of city outsiders. Others, Thembi and Jabulani among them, saw him as a criminal, a perversion of a tradition that was meant to be a respectful rite, not an act of force. The pride and power of Mkhulu's family, once unshakeable, now hung in the balance.

The legal battle was just beginning. Ms. Maseko informed Thabo that they would be filing charges of kidnapping and sexual assault. She explained that the 'bride price' Mkhulu had mentioned was a form of extortion, and that they would have to find a way to navigate the complex legal landscape where traditional customs and modern law often clashed. The road ahead, she warned, would be long and difficult.

Naledi, who had been a whirlwind of emotion in the first few days, now settled into a quiet, haunted silence. She went to her room, a space that had once been a sanctuary of teenage life, and looked at it with a strange detachment. Her school books, her posters of pop stars, her neatly organized closet—it all felt like a life she had once known, but no longer inhabited. She was still a fifteen-year-old girl, but a part of her had grown up in that dark hut, and that part of her was now demanding attention.

She lay in her bed at night, staring at the ceiling, replaying the words of Sipho and Mkhulu, the look on MaZondo's face, the terror of that dark walk to the compound. But she also replayed the memory of her parents' fierce love, of her own small, courageous voice that had finally said, "I want to go home." She had found a strength within herself she didn't know she had, a strength that had saved her.

The long road home was not just the physical distance between the village and the city. It was the emotional and psychological journey she was now on, a journey that would involve confronting her trauma, finding her voice, and understanding that her freedom was a gift she had fought for, and that she would have to fight for again. Her escape from the village was only the first step. The real fight, the one for justice and healing, had just begun.

CHAPTER 11: THE BATTLE OF TWO WORLDS

The legal battle began not with a bang, but with a mountain of paperwork. Ms. Maseko, with her keen legal mind and a deep sense of purpose, guided Thabo and Lerato through the labyrinthine process of filing formal charges. The initial report to the local police in the rural town had been a necessary first step, but now, with Naledi safe and the family united, they were moving to a more formal, decisive front. The city's legal system, with its cold precision and impersonal language, was now their weapon.

Thabo and Lerato spent days with Ms. Maseko, recounting every detail of the incident, from the first phone call to the final, tense moments in MaZondo's compound. Lerato's testimony was a mixture of a mother's fear and a woman's outrage, her voice trembling as she described the moment she saw her daughter in strange clothes, a stranger in her own skin. Thabo's account was a father's narrative of betrayal and a modern man's frustration with a system that seemed to have no place for his daughter's rights.

But the hardest part, the most emotionally draining, was Naledi's turn. Ms. Maseko, a woman who had seen the darkest corners of human nature, was gentle with her. She asked Naledi to tell her story, to speak her truth, in her own time. The process forced Naledi to relive the trauma, to vocalize the fear that she had been holding inside. She spoke of Sipho's deceptive charm, the chilling feeling of being taken, the silent terror of being held against her will. She described the hut, the strange lessons, and the overwhelming feeling of powerlessness.

Each word Naledi spoke was a small act of bravery, a defiant pushback against the people who had tried to silence her. But with each word, the memories became sharper, more real. The ghost of her trauma, which had been lurking in the shadows, now stood in the harsh light of a legal proceeding. She was no longer just Naledi, a city girl who had gone on holiday. She was a victim, a witness, and the most important voice in a case that was rapidly gaining momentum.

Back in the village, news of the lawsuit was a fresh wave of outrage. Mkhulu, once a respected elder, was now seen as a figure of defiance, a bulwark against the encroachment of city law. He and his family saw the charges not as a criminal matter, but as a direct assault on their culture. The community, already divided, now drew a line in the sand. Sipho was no longer just a boy who had taken a bride; he was a symbol, a protector of their heritage.

Sipho, for his part, seemed unable to grasp the gravity of the situation. He genuinely believed that what he had done was not a crime, but a rite of passage. He was a man, he had chosen his wife, and the 'bride price' had been paid. The city law, he reasoned, was for city people. He was a man of the land, and his laws were older, more powerful. His father, Mkhulu, fueled his sense of righteous indignation, assuring him that this was a battle they would win.

The fallout was particularly harsh for Thembi and Jabulani. Their decision to stand with Thabo and Lerato was seen as a betrayal of their own community. The villagers, once friendly and welcoming, now passed them with cold, silent stares. Their homestead, once a hub of activity, was now an island of isolation. They were ostracized, punished for their morality. Thembi, heartbroken, could only watch as the community she loved so deeply turned its back on her, a victim of a tribal war she had no desire to fight.

For Thabo and Lerato, the fight was a slow, exhausting drain on their lives. The legal fees were mounting, and the endless meetings and phone calls consumed their time and energy. But their resolve never wavered. They were a united front, a team of two, fighting for their daughter's right to a future she had almost lost. They had promised Naledi they would see this through, and they would not break that promise, no matter the cost.

The story, a microcosm of a much larger national debate, began to catch the attention of the media. A reporter from a national newspaper, intrigued by the case of "the city girl and the tribal tradition," reached out to Ms. Maseko. The story, once confined to the legal documents and hushed conversations, was now a public spectacle. The headline, "Custom or Crime? A Battle for a Young Girl's Freedom," was a jarring reminder that their private trauma had now become a public debate.

The media attention was a double-edged sword. It brought a renewed sense of urgency to the case, and it put pressure on the legal system to act. But it also brought a new kind of scrutiny. The comments sections of news articles were filled with heated debate, with people from all walks of life weighing in on the issue. Some were outraged by the abduction, calling it a blatant abuse of power. Others defended the tradition, arguing that city people had no right to interfere with their culture.

Naledi, who was just beginning to find her footing again, now had to face a new kind of terror: her face and her story were everywhere. Her quiet, internal battle had become a loud, public spectacle. She was no longer just Naledi. She was a symbol, a case study, a girl caught in the crossfire of a cultural war she didn't want to fight.

The fight, which had once felt like a simple battle to bring her home, was now a complex, multi-faceted war. It was a war for justice, a war for tradition, and a war for the right to choose her own destiny. The long road home was far from over. It had simply led her to a new, more dangerous battlefield, where the weapons were not spears and fists, but legal documents and public opinion.

Naledi, sitting in her room, looked at the phone that her parents had returned to her, a small, black rectangle that felt so different now.

It was no longer just a device for talking to friends. It was a symbol of her freedom, a lifeline to the world she had almost lost. She knew she could not go back to the girl she was before. She was a different person now, stronger, and more resolved than ever. She would fight, not just for herself, but for every girl who had ever been silenced.

CHAPTER 12: THE WEIGHT OF THE WORLD

The public spotlight, at first a distant flicker, now became a blinding, harsh glare. The single newspaper article had opened a Pandora's box of media attention. Naledi's face, once a private joy to her parents, was now plastered across news channels and social media feeds. She saw herself on television, a grainy photo from her last birthday, used to illustrate a story she was still struggling to understand herself. She was no longer Naledi; she was "the city girl," a symbol in a national debate, her trauma reduced to a headline.

For Naledi, this new reality was a terrifying extension of her captivity. In the village, her body had been held hostage. Now, her story was. She felt a profound sense of violation, a feeling that her most private fears were being dissected by strangers in comment sections and on talk shows. The debate was fierce and polarized. One side, a chorus of angry voices, condemned Sipho and Mkhulu as criminals and called for justice. The other, fueled by a deep-seated distrust of city values, defended *ukuthwala* as a sacred tradition under attack. Naledi found herself trapped in the crossfire of a war she hadn't started and never wanted to fight.

Thabo and Lerato worked tirelessly to shield their daughter from the onslaught. Lerato, with a mother's fierce instinct, turned off the television whenever a report came on and filtered all her online interactions. Thabo, working with Ms. Maseko, issued a statement to the press, asking for privacy and reminding them that a child's well-being was at stake. But the media machine was relentless.

Reporters lurked outside their apartment building, a constant, invasive presence. Their private pain had become a public spectacle, and the weight of the world felt heavy on their shoulders.

Back in the village, the media storm had a different effect. Mkhulu, once the quiet authority of his community, now saw his power challenged not by a single family, but by the entire nation. The television reports, showing his face and the faces of his fellow elders, were a source of deep shame and outrage. He saw himself as a man under siege, and the charges against his son as a cruel, political attack on their way of life. This was not about a girl, he reasoned; this was about the city trying to erase their culture.

Sipho, however, was emboldened. He was getting calls and messages from people in other villages who saw him as a hero, a young man who had stood his ground. He genuinely believed that the city media was lying, twisting his story to fit their narrative. He saw himself not as a kidnapper, but as a martyr, a man who was suffering for the honor of his ancestors. He was still convinced he had done nothing wrong, and the public outcry only solidified his sense of righteous indignation.

The one bridge between these two worlds was Thembi and Jabulani. Ostracized by their own community, they stood firm in their support of Naledi's family. Thembi, heartbroken by the rift, provided a vital source of information to Thabo and Lerato, keeping them informed of the village's mood and Mkhulu's plans. They were the lonely, moral compass in a world that had gone mad with pride and tradition. Their quiet loyalty became a wellspring of hope for a family that felt completely isolated.

In her room, Naledi sat with her returned phone, scrolling through the news articles and social media posts. She read the vitriol and the support, the arguments for and against her. At first, it was a paralyzing terror, but slowly, a new feeling began to take hold. She saw that her story was bigger than just her. It was a story that countless other girls, in countless other villages, had lived and would continue to live. She realized that by being silent, she was letting others tell her story for her.

The quiet, internal war she had been fighting gave way to a new kind of resolve. Her trauma had stripped her of her voice, but the public debate was forcing her to find it again. She was no longer just a victim. She was a witness, a survivor, and a symbol of something far greater than herself. She realized that if she wanted to change the world, she had to stop being a passive spectator in her own life. She had to take control of her narrative. She had to speak her truth, not just to the police or her family, but to everyone who was listening.

CHAPTER 13: FINDING HER VOICE

The resolve that had sparked in Naledi's mind was a fragile, yet powerful thing. The next morning, she approached her parents with a quiet certainty that surprised them both. They were in the kitchen, drinking coffee and trying to ignore the constant low murmur of the television news about their case. Naledi stood in the doorway, her arms crossed, and waited for them to notice her. When they did, she said, "I want to talk to the reporters."

Thabo and Lerato looked at each other, their faces a mixture of shock and terror. "Naledi, no," Thabo said immediately, his voice laced with the fear that had become a constant companion. "We've been trying to keep you out of this. It's too much. The media... they twist things." Lerato, her eyes wide with worry, took a step towards her daughter. "Your father is right, my love. We can't let them do this to you. We've done everything we can to shield you from the ugliness of all this."

But Naledi was firm. Her voice, once a small, terrified whisper, was now strong and clear. "I know. But they're twisting my story anyway. They're talking about 'the city girl' and 'the tribal tradition,' and no one is talking about me. No one is talking about what happened. They are fighting over me, and I am not even there. I want to be there. I want to tell them what it feels like." She looked at them, her eyes pleading for them to understand. "I want to be the one who tells my story."

The conviction in her voice was undeniable. They saw in her not a scared child, but a young woman who had been through a crucible and emerged with a steel core. After a long, quiet conversation, they called Ms. Maseko. The lawyer, a pragmatic woman who rarely showed emotion, was hesitant at first. "The media can be a minefield, Thabo," she warned. "It could jeopardize the case. But," she added, her voice softening, "if the girl is ready, a live testimony from the victim herself could be a very powerful thing. It could change the entire narrative."

The decision was made. The next day, Thabo and Lerato, with Naledi walking between them, her head held high, faced a sea of reporters outside their lawyer's office. Naledi's heart pounded, a frantic drum against her ribs. The camera flashes were like small, silent explosions, and the microphones, a forest of metal, seemed to reach out to her like hungry snakes. She stood at the podium, a small, fragile figure, but a wave of profound calm settled over her. This was not a performance. This was her truth.

She began to speak, her voice shaking at first, but then finding its rhythm. She did not speak in legal terms or in abstract cultural debates. She spoke as a fifteen-year-old girl. She spoke of her excitement to visit her relatives, of the warmth of Thembi's hug, of Sipho's deceiving smile. She spoke of the confusion, the terror, the feeling of being stripped of her identity. "I was not a bride," she said, her voice clear and ringing. "I was a child, and I was taken. No culture, no tradition, gives anyone the right to do that."

The effect was immediate and profound. The reporters, who had been a ravenous pack of wolves, fell silent. The debate, which had been a clash of ideologies, now had a human face, a human voice. The story was no longer about "the city girl" or "the tribal tradition." It was about Naledi. It was about a child who had been wronged, and who had found the courage to speak out. The video of her statement went viral, spreading across social media and news sites like wildfire. The outrage, once a polarized debate, now coalesced into a single, unified roar for justice.

In the village, the news hit like a devastating blow. Mkhulu watched the video on his small, portable television, his face a mask of disbelief and fury. Naledi was no longer a symbol; she was a girl, speaking her truth, and her truth was a direct challenge to his authority. He saw his world crumbling, his power slipping away, not to the law, but to the brave, honest words of a child he had tried to silence.

Sipho, however, was in a state of utter denial. He watched the video and saw not a victim, but a liar, a traitor. He believed she was being forced to say these things by her parents and the city media. His sense of martyrdom only deepened, and his rage, once a low hum of indignation, now sharpened into a bitter hatred. He saw himself as a man who had not only lost his bride, but had been publicly shamed for doing what he believed was right. He wanted revenge.

The fallout was also felt by Thembi and Jabulani. The video of Naledi's speech, which had made them so proud, also made them a target. The village's anger, fueled by Mkhulu and Sipho, was now directed at them, a constant barrage of cold stares and whispered insults. But their resolve held firm. They had chosen a side, and they would not back down, no matter the cost.

For Naledi, the public statement was a turning point. It did not magically heal her trauma, but it gave her a sense of power, a feeling that she was no longer a victim, but a survivor. She had taken control of her story, and in doing so, she had found her voice. The long, difficult journey was far from over. But for the first time since that day on the koppie, Naledi felt a profound sense of hope.

CHAPTER 14: THE CRACKDOWN

Naledi's powerful testimony was a spark that ignited a fire. The viral video, a raw and unflinching account of her trauma, left no room for doubt or debate. It was no longer a story of cultural difference; it was a clear case of a child's rights being violated. The public outcry was deafening, and the legal system, once hesitant, now moved with a swift and focused purpose. The case was elevated, assigned to a no-nonsense prosecutor, and a warrant for the arrest of Sipho and Mkhulu was issued. The law had finally come for them.

The arrival of the police in the village this time was not a quiet, tentative visit. Two police vans, sirens wailing, pulled up to Mkhulu's compound, a jarring spectacle of flashing blue and red that shattered the morning's peaceful quiet. A dozen officers, led by Sergeant Dube, now a man on a mission, fanned out across the yard. The villagers, who had gathered outside, watched in a stunned silence. This was not a discussion; this was an operation.

Mkhulu emerged from his hut, his face a mask of defiant fury. "What is the meaning of this?" he demanded, his voice a low, dangerous rumble. "You have no right to come here, to treat us like common criminals!" Sergeant Dube, his face grim, held up the warrant. "Mkhulu, you are under arrest for your role in the kidnapping of Naledi and for obstructing justice. Sipho, your son, is also under arrest for kidnapping and assault." The words, spoken in the language of the law, were a foreign invader in their world.

Sipho, dragged from his hut by two officers, was in a state of utter disbelief. His triumphant smile from the day before was gone, replaced by a look of sheer, unadulterated hatred. He saw his world, his destiny, his very honor, being torn to pieces by these men in uniforms. He looked at the villagers, the women who had once supported him now looking on in silent terror, and he felt a profound sense of betrayal. He was not a criminal; he was a martyr. He was a hero, and they were all letting this happen.

As the officers led Sipho and Mkhulu away, the village erupted. The women began to wail, a communal cry of grief and anger. The men shouted insults and threats at the police vans as they drove away. The fragile truce of tradition had been broken, and in its place, a bitter, seething hatred had taken root. Thembi and Jabulani watched from their homestead, their hearts heavy with a mixture of relief and fear. The battle was won, but the war, they knew, was far from over.

Back in the city, Naledi watched the news reports of the arrests, a strange, hollow feeling settling in her stomach. The arrests were a victory, a final act of justice. But the sight of Sipho's face, contorted with rage and hatred, sent a shiver down her spine. The boy she had once thought of as a friend was gone, replaced by a monster. The part of her that wanted to see him punished was satisfied, but the part that had known him was left with a deep, unsettling sense of sorrow.

With the arrests made, the legal process shifted to a new phase. Ms. Maseko began preparing for the trial, confident in her case but wary of the political and cultural landmines that lay ahead. The legal team was strong, the evidence was clear, and with Naledi's testimony, they had a powerful emotional weapon. But Mkhulu's threats and the village's anger were not to be taken lightly. The trial would be a public spectacle, a clash of two worlds on a courtroom stage.

Naledi, now a figure of national fame, began to use her new platform for good. She was invited to speak at a local women's shelter, where she met other girls who had been victims of similar circumstances. She found a new purpose in telling her story, not just as a survivor, but as a voice for the voiceless. She spoke of her fear, her courage, and her hope for a future where no girl would have to go through what she had. Her trauma had given her a mission, a cause that would define her life.

The road to healing was a slow and deliberate one. The nightmares were less frequent, the fear was less intense, but the scars remained. Naledi began seeing a therapist, a kind and patient woman who helped her navigate the complex emotional landscape of her trauma. She was learning to live with her past, not as a victim, but as a survivor. She was still a fifteen-year-old girl, but she was a different person now, stronger and more resilient than ever before.

Thabo and Lerato, for their part, were finally beginning to breathe again. The fear that had been their constant companion had been replaced by a quiet sense of purpose. They were no longer just a mother and father fighting for their child; they were a family, a unit, working together to see that justice was done. Their life had been changed forever, but in a way, it had also been strengthened. They had faced a darkness they had never imagined, and they had emerged, together, on the other side.

The arrests were a victory, but the battle was far from over. The legal proceedings were just beginning, and Mkhulu and Sipho, now behind bars, were not defeated. Mkhulu's threats of "consequences" and Sipho's burning rage were a dark cloud hanging over their family, a promise of a reckoning to come. Naledi had faced her captors and won, but she knew in her heart that the most dangerous part of her journey, the one where she would have to face the long and bitter fallout of her fight for freedom, was just beginning.

CHAPTER 15: THE TRIAL BEGINS

The arrests of Sipho and Mkhulu were a temporary victory, but they were far from the end of the war. They had been taken into custody, but their influence and power had not been so easily contained. From behind bars, Mkhulu, a man of profound pride and deep connections, was still orchestrating his defense. He hired a high-profile lawyer, a charismatic man named Mr. Xhosa, who specialized in cases involving traditional law. Their strategy was clear: frame the entire incident not as a criminal act, but as a cultural misunderstanding, a clash between the city's secular laws and the sacred, time-honored customs of the village.

Ms. Maseko, with her pragmatic legal mind, was prepared for this. She spent hours with Naledi, preparing her for the courtroom. She explained that the defense would try to discredit her, to portray her not as a victim, but as a rebellious city girl who had willfully disobeyed the traditions of her people. They would likely paint Naledi's public testimony as a staged performance, a calculated attempt to smear an entire community. Naledi listened, her face grim, her newfound courage hardening into a steel resolve. She was ready to face them again, this time on a different kind of battlefield.

The media, which had been so quick to champion Naledi, was now a constant, buzzing presence, eager for every detail of the impending trial. News channels ran segments on the history of *ukuthwala*, with legal and cultural experts debating the nuances of the custom. The debate, which had briefly united the nation in outrage, now fractured along familiar lines. The city versus the rural. Modernity versus tradition. Naledi's story was no longer just her own; it was a symbol, a lightning rod for a nation grappling with its own identity.

For Naledi, the preparations for the trial were an intense, emotional ordeal. Each meeting with Ms. Maseko was a step back into her trauma, a forced reliving of the fear and the loneliness. She had to learn to speak with clinical detachment, to recall facts and not feelings. But her parents were her rock, her unwavering support system. Lerato was a constant presence, her silent strength a balm to Naledi's wounded spirit. Thabo, for his part, was a man of action, a quiet force of nature, ensuring every detail was taken care of.

Back in the village, the atmosphere was one of quiet hostility and deep-seated fear. Mkhulu's family, now without their patriarch, was a source of pity and respect. They were seen as martyrs, their sacrifice a testament to their unwavering faith in the old ways. Thembi and Jabulani, who had sided with Naledi's family, were still ostracized, their homestead a lonely outpost in a village that had turned its back on them. They were paying a heavy price for their morality, a price that they were willing to pay.

The one person who seemed to be thriving in the chaos was Sipho. From his prison cell, he was in a state of utter denial. He had his own lawyer, a young, idealistic man who saw him as a victim of a cruel, unjust system. Sipho genuinely believed that he was being persecuted, that his innocence would be proven, and that Naledi, the girl he still saw as his bride, would one day see the truth. His hatred for her, and for the city that had stolen her from him, was a consuming fire, a bitter poison that would fuel his every action.

Finally, the day of the trial arrived. The courtroom was packed, a sea of reporters, concerned citizens, and lawyers from both sides. Naledi, dressed in a simple, elegant suit, sat between her parents and Ms. Maseko, her face a mask of calm determination. She looked across the courtroom, her eyes falling on Sipho and Mkhulu. Sipho, now in a suit, his face pale, met her gaze with a cold, unyielding stare. Mkhulu, in his traditional attire, looked at her not with hatred, but with a profound and chilling contempt, as if she were a ghost from a future he refused to acknowledge.

The judge, a stern-faced woman with an aura of quiet authority, called the court to order. Ms. Maseko, in her opening statement, laid out the case in a clear, concise manner, describing the kidnapping not as a cultural rite, but as a criminal act. Mr. Xhosa, for the defense, responded with a passionate, emotional argument about the sanctity of tradition and the importance of a community's right to self-governance. The battle lines were drawn. The trial, a spectacle that would hold the nation's attention for weeks, had begun.

CHAPTER 16: THE WITNESS STAND

The first day of the trial was a torrent of legal formalities and procedural battles. Ms. Maseko, with her clinical precision, presented a timeline of events, supported by police reports and forensic evidence. Mr. Xhosa, the defense lawyer for Mkhulu and Sipho, countered with a series of motions, arguing for a mistrial on the grounds of cultural bias and a violation of traditional rights. The judge, a woman who seemed to be a master of the delicate art of balancing the law with an understanding of social complexities, denied his motions, and the stage was set for the trial's first, and most crucial, witness: Naledi.

Naledi, who had been sitting with her parents, felt a cold knot of dread tighten in her stomach as her name was called. She walked to the witness stand, a small, fragile figure in a large, imposing room. The entire courtroom seemed to hold its breath. She took the oath, her voice a barely audible whisper, and sat down. Her eyes, however, were not on the judge, or the jury, or even on her parents. They were fixed on Sipho and Mkhulu, a silent defiance in her gaze that spoke volumes.

Ms. Maseko began her questioning with a gentle, reassuring tone, guiding Naledi through her story. Naledi spoke of her excitement to visit her family, the warmth of Thembi's welcome, and the genuine joy of reconnecting with her roots. But as she spoke of the day of the abduction, her voice trembled with emotion. She described the walk to the "waterfall," the sudden, chilling realization of Sipho's betrayal, and the terror of being held against her will. She recounted the long nights in the hut, the pressure to conform, and the feeling of being stripped of her identity.

When Ms. Maseko finished, the courtroom was a picture of hushed shock and sympathy. Naledi's testimony had been raw, honest, and devastatingly effective. But now it was Mr. Xhosa's turn. He approached the stand with a confident, almost theatrical stride, his smile a thin, disarming line. "Naledi," he began, his voice smooth and friendly, "you say you were taken against your will. But isn't it true that you had a very good time in the village? That you were laughing and talking with my client, Sipho? That you went on a walk with him of your own free will?"

His questions were a barrage of subtle attacks, a slow, methodical attempt to chip away at her credibility. He painted a picture of a romantic interest, a young girl who was eager to spend time with a handsome boy. He suggested that her protests were a result of her city upbringing, a childish rebellion against a cultural rite she didn't understand. He brought up her city clothes, her education, her friends, all as evidence of her "disrespect for tradition."

But Naledi, prepared for this, held firm. Her fear was still there, a constant hum beneath the surface, but her resolve was a shield. She looked at Mr. Xhosa, her eyes blazing with a newfound courage. "I liked spending time with Sipho," she said, her voice clear and strong. "But I never agreed to be his wife. And no matter how much fun I was having, it doesn't give him the right to take me." She looked at the jury, her gaze unwavering. "I was a child. I was a guest. I was a person, and I had a right to say no."

The retort, simple and powerful, landed like a punch. Mr. Xhosa's smile faltered, but he quickly recovered, changing his tack. He spoke of the bride price, a payment made to the community that symbolized her acceptance into the family. Naledi, however, was ready. "A bride price is for a woman who chooses to be a wife," she said. "I was a child. I was not a woman. And I did not choose." She had used the language of the culture against them, a final, definitive rebuttal.

From across the courtroom, Thabo and Lerato watched with a mix of pride and agony. They saw their daughter not as a victim, but as a warrior, fighting her own battle. They saw Sipho, his face a mask of rage and humiliation, and Mkhulu, whose initial contempt had been replaced by a look of profound, chilling hatred. The contempt, Naledi realized, had been the contempt of a man who saw a child. The hatred was for a woman who had spoken her truth and challenged his world.

The trial was adjourned for the day. Naledi walked from the courtroom, her head held high, with her parents and Ms. Maseko surrounding her. She had faced them. She had spoken her truth. The victory was a small one, but it was a victory nonetheless. The long road to justice was still ahead, but for the first time since that day on the koppie, Naledi felt a profound and powerful sense of peace. She had been silenced, but she had found her voice, and she had used it to speak not just for herself, but for every girl who had ever been a victim.

CHAPTER 17: THE AFTERMATH OF TRUTH

The air outside the courtroom was different. The media, a pack of hungry wolves just moments before, now stood in a respectful, hushed circle. The questions they shouted were no longer aggressive demands but quiet inquiries about Naledi's well-being. The raw power of her testimony had disarmed them all. Naledi, with her parents on either side and Ms. Maseko at her back, walked through the throng of reporters like a queen leaving her throne. She was exhausted, but a profound sense of calm had settled over her, a feeling she hadn't experienced since before the bus ride to the village.

In the car, the silence was heavy but not oppressive. It was the silence of shared relief, of a battle fought and won, at least for the day. Lerato reached over and gently took Naledi's hand. "You were so brave, my love," she whispered, her voice thick with emotion. Thabo, driving with a quiet, focused intensity, simply nodded, a single tear rolling down his cheek. Naledi looked from one parent to the other, seeing in their faces not just love, but a deep, unwavering pride that felt like a healing balm to her wounded spirit.

Back at their apartment, the tension of the last few weeks finally began to dissipate. Naledi, for the first time, felt truly safe. She took a long, hot shower, washing away not just the dust of the courtroom but the lingering fear of the past months. Her parents ordered a celebratory dinner, and they sat together, laughing and talking about everything and nothing. It was a moment of pure, unadulterated family joy, a small, precious victory in a war that was far from over.

Meanwhile, in a high-rise office overlooking the city, Mr. Xhosa was in a state of controlled fury. Naledi's testimony had been a disaster for his case. She was not the rebellious city girl he had hoped to portray; she was a compelling, articulate victim whose simple truth had completely dismantled his entire defense. He had expected a child; he had faced a warrior. He slammed his fist on his desk. He needed a new plan. He needed a way to restore the narrative, to shift the focus back to the "sanctity of tradition."

He immediately called Mkhulu, who was now out on bail, his face a mask of bitter resentment. Mr. Xhosa outlined his new strategy. They would not attack Naledi's character directly. Instead, they would call a series of witnesses from the village—elders and community members who would testify to the sacredness of the *ukuthwala* custom. They would speak of its historical context, its importance to their lineage, and its place in the community. He would turn the trial into a debate on cultural heritage itself.

Back in the village, the news of Naledi's testimony and the arrests of Mkhulu and Sipho had a profound and lasting effect. The community was no longer just divided; it was shattered. Some villagers, seeing the raw emotion in Naledi's testimony, began to question the old ways, wondering if a tradition that could cause so much pain was truly a tradition worth defending. Others, however, stood firmly with Mkhulu, seeing his arrest not as justice, but as an attack on their entire way of life.

The fallout was particularly difficult for Thembi and Jabulani. The scorn and isolation they had experienced before now intensified, fueled by Mkhulu's threats and the village's anger. But they remained resolute. Thembi, watching the news reports of Naledi's bravery, felt a deep sense of pride. She had been right to stand with her niece. Her quiet sense of morality, once a lonely island, now felt like a firm and unshakeable foundation in a sea of chaos.

For Naledi, the day was not just a victory but a turning point. She had been a victim of a crime, but she had also been the catalyst for a larger conversation. Her voice, once silenced, was now a powerful force for change. The trial was far from over. She knew that Mr. Xhosa would come back with a new, more dangerous line of attack. But for the first time, she wasn't afraid. She had faced her demons and spoken her truth. She was a survivor, and she was ready for the next battle.

CHAPTER 18: THE OLD WAYS TESTIFY

The courtroom, once a place of somber focus, was now a stage for a grander, more complicated drama. Mr. Xhosa's strategy to turn the case into a debate on cultural heritage had worked. He had called a series of witnesses, not from the city, but from the heart of the village. The atmosphere shifted palpably as the first of them, a man with a weathered face and a quiet dignity, walked to the stand. This was not a legal battle anymore; it was a clash of civilizations.

The witnesses, one after another, spoke with a deep, unwavering conviction. They were not liars; they were true believers. They spoke of the sanctity of *ukuthwala*, not as a crime, but as a revered custom that had held their community together for generations. They spoke of lineage, of the importance of a woman's role in securing the future of her family, and of the sacred traditions passed down from their ancestors. They painted a picture of a world where honor was everything, and a promise was a binding contract between families.

Each word they spoke was a dagger in Naledi's heart. She watched them, her face a mask of quiet torment, as they dismantled her world. They spoke of her parents not as loving protectors, but as misguided city people who had forgotten their roots. They spoke of Thabo as a man who had abandoned his culture and his people, a man who had brought a foreign law to a sacred place. They spoke of Naledi's city life—her education, her independence—as a source of her "rebellion," a corruption of a spirit that was meant to be pure and dedicated to her community.

Thabo, sitting beside his daughter, felt the weight of their words like a physical blow. The guilt he had been carrying for weeks, a quiet hum beneath the surface of his rage, now erupted into a sharp, bitter pain. He had left this world to protect his daughter from its darker side, but now the world he had left behind was using that very act as a weapon against them. He wanted to shout, to stand up and scream that his love for his daughter was not a sign of his weakness, but of his strength. But his lawyer held him back, a quiet hand on his arm, a silent command to hold his fire.

Lerato, for her part, was a silent fury. She watched as these strangers, people who had never met her, dissected her family's choices. She saw the jury, their faces a mixture of confusion and sympathy, trying to navigate the two competing narratives. She felt a profound sense of helplessness as she watched their family, their values, their entire way of life, being put on trial. This was not about justice anymore; it was about pride, tradition, and the deep, unyielding power of a community under siege.

Ms. Maseko, however, was not intimidated. She was a master of her craft, and she saw the witnesses not as people, but as legal challenges. She cross-examined them with a cool, detached professionalism, not by attacking their beliefs, but by questioning their methods. She asked them if a child could truly consent to a lifetime of marriage. She asked them if a community's right to tradition superseded a child's right to safety. She forced them to admit that what had happened to Naledi was not just a rite of passage, but a use of force.

The cross-examination was a brilliant display of legal acrobatics, but it was not enough. The defense's narrative, of a community wronged by city people, was a powerful and emotional one. The trial had become a grand, philosophical debate, and the jury, caught in the crossfire, was now more confused than ever. The simple, raw truth of Naledi's story, which had once been so clear, was now buried under a mountain of tradition, pride, and legal argument.

As the day came to a close, Naledi walked from the courtroom, her body heavy with the weight of her ancestors. She had faced her kidnapper and won. She had faced her community and spoken her truth. But now, she was facing something far more terrifying: a world that was telling her she was wrong to want to be free. The battle for justice was now a battle for her soul, and the outcome, once so certain, now hung in the balance.

CHAPTER 19: THE VERDICT

The jury's deliberation room was a crucible of conflicting ideas. The simple truth of Naledi's testimony, so powerful and raw, was pitted against the deep, unwavering conviction of the village elders. The jurors, a cross-section of the nation's people, were caught between two competing worlds—the law of the land and the law of tradition. The hours stretched into days, and the air in the courtroom became thick with a heavy, palpable tension. Every legal pundit on television offered a different prediction, but no one could truly know the inner workings of the jury's mind.

On the final day, the courtroom was packed to capacity, a sea of anxious faces. Naledi, her parents, and Ms. Maseko sat in a tight, silent huddle, their hands clasped together. They had done everything they could. The rest was up to the system. Across the aisle, Mkhulu and Sipho sat with Mr. Xhosa, their faces a mask of quiet defiance. Sipho, now a public figure of controversy, still held a flicker of hope in his eyes, a profound belief that he would be exonerated. Mkhulu, however, was a man who knew the tide of a battle was turning. His fury had hardened into a cold, menacing resolve.

Finally, a bailiff announced the jury had reached a verdict. The courtroom, which had been buzzing with hushed conversations, fell into a profound and chilling silence. The jurors filed in, their faces giving nothing away, a dozen blank slates carrying the weight of a nation's hopes and fears. Naledi's heart pounded, a frantic drum against her ribs. She looked at her mother, who gave her a reassuring squeeze on the hand, and at her father, whose jaw was set in a grim line.

The judge, her face a neutral mask of authority, asked the jury foreman to stand. The foreman, a woman with kind eyes and a serious demeanor, held up a single piece of paper. The air in the courtroom seemed to thin, every single person holding their breath, waiting for the words that would change everything.

"On the charge of kidnapping," the foreman's voice was clear and unwavering, "we the jury, find the defendant, Sipho, guilty."

A collective gasp rippled through the courtroom, followed by the muffled sobs of Lerato and the quiet, triumphant tears of Thabo. Naledi felt a sudden, profound rush of relief, a wave of emotion that was so strong it almost brought her to her knees. She had done it. Her truth had been heard. Justice had prevailed.

The foreman continued, her voice still ringing with authority. "On the charge of kidnapping, we the jury, find the defendant, Mkhulu, guilty."

This time, the reaction was different. Mkhulu, the patriarch of a proud family, a man who had believed his customs were a shield against the law, simply closed his eyes, his face a mask of bitter, profound defeat. Sipho, his triumphant hope shattered, lunged forward with a roar of pure, unadulterated rage, his face contorted in a chilling expression of betrayal. It took two bailiffs to hold him back, his shouts echoing through the silent courtroom.

The judge, her face now grim, slammed her gavel down. "Order!" she commanded. "I have heard the verdict, and I will now pass sentence." She then spoke of the sanctity of the law, of the protection of children, and of the importance of a nation's laws being applied equally to all, regardless of tradition. She sentenced Sipho to a lengthy prison term, a punishment for his crime and a message to the nation. Mkhulu, for his role in obstructing justice and enabling the crime, also received a sentence.

The verdict was more than just a legal outcome; it was a watershed moment. The media, which had been so divided, now coalesced into a single voice of triumph. Naledi, a girl who had gone on a holiday and found herself in a nightmare, was now a national hero, a symbol of courage and a beacon of hope for countless other girls. The law had stood firm, and in doing so, it had sent a clear and unequivocal message: tradition could not be used as a shield for crime.

As they left the courtroom, Naledi looked at her parents, her eyes filled with a new, profound sense of peace. The verdict was a victory, but she knew it was not the end. The emotional scars would take time to heal. The nightmares would likely linger. But the fear, the terror, the feeling of powerlessness, had been replaced by a quiet sense of triumph. She had faced her kidnappers, she had spoken her truth, and she had won. Her long, difficult journey was finally, truly, over.

CHAPTER 20: AFTERMATH AND A NEW DAWN

The verdict echoed long after the judge's gavel fell, a powerful sound that reverberated not just in the courtroom, but across the nation. For Naledi, the years that followed were a journey of quiet healing. The legal victory was a crucial step, but it was only the first on a long road to recovery. The media attention eventually faded, the headlines moved on to other stories, and Naledi was finally able to reclaim her life from the public stage.

She returned to school, a place that had once been a source of simple joy, now a sanctuary of normalcy. She was no longer just "the girl from the trial." She was a student, a friend, and a young woman with a future of her own making. The emotional scars remained, a quiet presence in her life, but she learned to live with them, not as a victim, but as a survivor. She found a new passion in law and advocacy, inspired by Ms. Maseko's unwavering support and her own experience. She realized that her voice, once silenced, had the power to help others. She would one day fight for other girls who had been caught in the crossfire of tradition and injustice.

For Thabo and Lerato, the verdict was a hard-won peace. The fear that had been their constant companion had finally been replaced by a sense of calm. They had faced a darkness they never imagined, and they had emerged, together, a family unit stronger and more united than ever. They were no longer just a mother and father; they were a family of warriors, who had fought a long, difficult war for the soul of their daughter and won.

In the village, the fallout was severe and lasting. The legal precedent set by the trial, a clear and unequivocal message that tradition could not be used as a shield for crime, sent shockwaves through the community. Some elders, humbled by the verdict and the public shame, began to openly question the darker sides of *ukuthwala*, advocating for a modernization of the custom to ensure the consent and safety of girls. Others, however, clung to the old ways with a fierce, bitter resentment, seeing the verdict as a final, cruel act of city interference.

Thembi and Jabulani, who had risked everything for their family, found themselves at the center of a new, fractured community. They were ostracized by many but also became symbols of moral courage to a new generation of villagers who were beginning to question the customs of their ancestors. Their stand for what was right had cost them dearly, but in doing so, they had planted the seeds of change in their community, a slow, quiet revolution that would take years to bear fruit.

Mkhulu, released from prison, returned to the village a defeated man. His power and influence, once absolute, had been irreparably damaged. He was still an elder, but his authority was now a hollow shell. He had lost his son to the city's law, and his reputation to a girl's courage. His once-unshakable pride had been broken, replaced by a quiet and profound bitterness. He had fought a battle and lost not to a stronger army, but to the simple truth of a child's heart.

And Sipho, from his prison cell, never found peace. He believed his innocence would one day be proven, his destiny as a husband and a patriarch fulfilled. But as the years turned into a long, lonely sentence, his righteous indignation turned into a bitter rage. He was a man who had not just lost his freedom but had lost his soul in a war he had started, a war he had truly believed he was meant to win. He had been a hero in his own story, but the world had seen him for what he truly was: a criminal.

Years later, Naledi, now a young woman, sat with her parents on the anniversary of the trial. The nightmares were gone, the memories of the hut a distant, muted echo. She had just finished her first year of law school, and she was writing a paper on the intersection of traditional law and a child's rights. She looked at her parents, their faces etched with the lines of age and worry, but also with a quiet pride that felt like the deepest kind of love. The journey had been long, the road difficult, but they had walked it together. Naledi, a girl who had been taken, had found her voice, reclaimed her life, and found a new purpose. She was not just a survivor; she was a beacon of hope, a new dawn for countless others.

CHAPTER 21: A LEGACY OF CHANGE

It was a cold, bright morning, ten years after the trial that had changed Naledi's life and the laws of a nation. Naledi, now a confident young woman in her mid-twenties, stood on a familiar hill overlooking the village. The air was crisp, carrying the scent of dry grass and woodsmoke, a smell that once triggered a cold fear in her, but now felt like a distant, muted echo. She was no longer just the "city girl" who had come here for a holiday; she was a law student, an intern at a women's rights organization, and a quiet, powerful advocate for change. She had returned to the village not as a victim, but as a messenger of a new dawn.

The village itself had changed, a slow, quiet revolution that had taken root in the fertile ground of justice. The homesteads were still the same, the rhythm of life still governed by the sun and the seasons, but a new spirit had taken hold. A small women's center, built with funds from a national organization, stood on the outskirts of the village. It offered legal advice, education, and, most importantly, a safe space for young girls to speak their minds. The custom of *ukuthwala* had not disappeared, but it had been irrevocably altered. It was now a respectful rite that required a girl's consent, a custom governed not by force, but by choice. The seeds of change Thembi and Jabulani had planted had finally taken root.

Naledi drove her own car, a small, practical vehicle that felt like a symbol of her independence, to the women's center. Thembi and Jabulani were there to greet her, their faces etched with the lines of age, but their eyes still sparkling with the same kindness and strength she remembered. Thembi held her in a long, warm embrace. "You came back," she whispered, her voice thick with emotion. "I knew you would." Naledi smiled, her heart full. "I had to," she said. "This is where the story began. I had to see where it was going."

They talked for hours, Thembi telling her of the slow, difficult process of change in the village. They had faced resistance, anger, and resentment, but they had never given up. She spoke of the young girls who now came to the center, their faces bright with hope, their futures no longer tied to the whim of a custom, but to the promise of their own dreams. Thembi's voice, once a quiet whisper of dissent, was now a powerful force of change in her community.

Later that day, Naledi sat with her parents on a koppie overlooking the village. Her father, Thabo, his hair now streaked with grey, sat quietly beside her. "We were so afraid for you," he said, his voice soft. "We thought we had lost you." Naledi took his hand, her fingers tracing the lines of worry and love on his. "You never lost me, Papa," she said. "You found me. You showed me what it meant to fight for what was right."

Lerato, sitting on her other side, simply held her hand, a silent but profound expression of the love and pride that had been the anchor of their family through it all. She had watched Naledi heal, grow, and blossom into the woman she was meant to be, a woman with a purpose that was bigger than herself. The trauma was a part of her story, but it was not her whole story. It had been the fire that had forged her, not the one that had destroyed her.

As the sun began to set, casting a deep orange glow over the hills, Naledi looked at the village one last time. She thought of Sipho, still in prison, his rage and his victimhood a self-inflicted prison that would likely never end. She thought of Mkhulu, a ghost of his former self, who had lost a war he had believed was his destiny to win. She felt a profound sense of sorrow for them, for the tragedy of lives built on a foundation of pride and tradition that had crumbled in the face of a single girl's courage.

But the sorrow was not the final note. It was a single, minor key in a symphony of hope. She looked at her parents, their faces glowing in the setting sun, and felt a profound sense of gratitude. She had lost her innocence, but she had gained a purpose. She had been a victim, but she had become a survivor. She had been silenced, but she had found her voice and used it to bring about a new dawn. Naledi, a girl who had been taken, had come home to a village, and a world, that was finally ready to listen.

CHAPTER 22: THE CONTINUING STRUGGLE

Five more years had passed since Naledi's return to the village. She was now a junior lawyer at a prestigious firm in the city, but her heart remained tied to the cause that had shaped her. She specialized in cases that intersected with traditional law, her own experience giving her a profound empathy and a fierce determination. She had successfully represented several young women from various rural communities, using the precedent of her own trial to challenge outdated customs and protect their rights. She was an attorney, but more than that, she was a symbol of hope.

One Friday, she packed a bag and made the familiar drive back to the village, a journey that no longer felt like a return to a haunted past, but a trip home. The women's center, once a small, fledgling operation, was now a thriving hub of activity. It had a small library, a computer lab, and a full-time staff of lawyers and social workers. Naledi had been instrumental in its growth, and she now served as its legal counsel, traveling to the village once a month to offer pro-bono services.

She found Thembi and Jabulani sitting outside their homestead, now surrounded by a new generation of children who looked up to them as quiet heroes. Thembi's face, etched with age, broke into a warm smile as she saw Naledi. "You came," she said, her voice full of a quiet joy. "We were hoping you would." Naledi sat with them, feeling a deep sense of peace. The struggle had been worth it. Their courage had not been in vain.

But the peace was a fragile thing. Thembi explained the new challenge they were facing. While the custom of *ukuthwala* had been largely reformed, a new, more subtle form of resistance was taking hold. A new generation of boys, fueled by the bitter resentment of their fathers and the insidious poison of social media, was beginning to push back. They were not using force, but manipulation. They were using threats, emotional blackmail, and a subtle but powerful form of social pressure to get what they wanted.

"They say that we have forgotten our traditions," Thembi said, her voice filled with a weary sadness. "They say that these girls are too free, that they have forgotten their place. They are not like Sipho. They are more clever. They use the city's ways against us." She spoke of girls being shamed online, their reputations destroyed by rumors and lies. She spoke of boys who believed that the legal victory was an injustice, a cruel act of city interference.

Naledi listened, her face grim. She realized that the fight was a never-ending cycle, a constant battle between progress and tradition, between freedom and control. She had thought that her legal victory had been the final chapter. But it had only been the beginning. Her work was not just about changing the law; it was about changing the hearts and minds of a generation.

The next day, she held a community meeting at the women's center. She spoke not as a lawyer, but as a survivor, a woman who had walked the path these girls were now walking. She spoke of the power of their voices, of the importance of knowing their rights, and of the strength of their own choices. The girls listened, their faces a mixture of fear and newfound resolve. She saw in their eyes the same fire she had once found in herself.

As the meeting ended, a young girl, no older than fifteen, approached her. Her name was Zola, and her eyes were filled with a quiet determination. "Thank you," she said, her voice soft. "My father, he still talks about the old ways. He says that we are bringing shame to our family. But I want to go to school. I want to be a teacher." Naledi looked at the girl and saw her own reflection—a child caught between two worlds, fighting for a future she had a right to claim.

Naledi smiled, a deep and genuine expression of hope. She took the girl's hand, a silent promise between them. The fight was not over. The legal battles were just beginning. But as she looked at the new generation of girls, she knew that the seeds of change had taken root. They had a voice, they had a choice, and they had a future. She would be there to help them every step of the way. She was not just a lawyer; she was a legacy.

CHAPTER 23: THE KIND OF BATTLE

Naledi's conversation with Zola was a quiet but profound turning point. The girl's plea, "I want to be a teacher," echoed the very core of Naledi's own fight for freedom. The challenge she faced now was more insidious than a simple kidnapping; it was a battle for the hearts and minds of an entire generation. She couldn't arrive with a police escort or a legal summons. Her weapons had to be persuasion, empathy, and the slow, steady power of a unified community.

The next day, she went with Thembi to Zola's homestead. They found Zola's father, a man named Khaya, sitting outside, carving a piece of wood. He was a man of quiet dignity, but his face was set in a hard, resolute line. He looked at Naledi with a mixture of respect and suspicion, a man who saw her not just as a person, but as the city's most powerful agent of change. "You have come for my daughter," he said, his voice quiet but firm. "You have come to turn her against her family, like you have done with so many others."

Naledi looked at him, not with anger, but with a deep understanding. "I have not come to turn her against you, Khaya," she said, her voice soft. "I have come to ensure her a future. I was once a girl like Zola. I wanted to learn, to grow, to see the world. My father, Thabo, understood this. He did not lose me to the city. He gained me as a woman who could stand on her own feet and make him proud."

She spoke not of the law, but of a father's love. She spoke of her own journey, of the pride she saw in her parents' eyes, and of the power of a family that supports its children's dreams. She didn't threaten him with legal action; she showed him a different path, a new kind of legacy. She spoke of the young men in the village who were using social media to shame girls, a betrayal of the very community they claimed to protect. "This is not our tradition," she said. "Our tradition is one of honor, not of cowardice. Our tradition is one of pride, not of cruelty."

Khaya listened, his hands still on the wood carving, but his eyes fixed on Naledi's face. He saw not a city lawyer, but a woman who had come home, a woman who spoke his language and understood his world. Her words were a mirror, showing him not just the danger his daughter faced, but the path he could take to protect her. He looked at Thembi, who simply nodded, a silent testament to the truth of Naledi's words.

After a long, quiet pause, Khaya looked at Naledi, a new expression in his eyes, a look of profound respect. "My daughter," he said, his voice a low whisper. "She wants to be a teacher." Naledi smiled, a deep and genuine expression of hope. "Yes," she said. "And she can be. With your support, she can be anything she wants." The words, so simple and yet so powerful, hung in the air. A new kind of agreement had been reached, a new kind of battle won.

The success of their conversation spread through the village like a quiet hum. Naledi's new strategy—using empathy and dialogue instead of legal force—was working. She held more community meetings, not in the women's center, but in the heart of the village, on the very ground that had once been the stage for her abduction. She spoke with young men, not as an enemy, but as a sister, a friend, a person who had seen the other side and wanted to help them find a better way.

The struggle was far from over. The old wounds were deep, the resentment still bitter. But for the first time since the verdict, Naledi saw a new kind of hope. The children of the village, the girls who had once been victims and the boys who had once been perpetrators, were now looking at each other not as enemies, but as partners in a new and different future. Naledi, a lawyer who had come home, was not just fighting for justice; she was fighting for a new kind of peace, a peace that was built not on force, but on the quiet, profound power of understanding.

CHAPTER 24: THE NEW ECHO OF RESENTMENT

The quiet victories Naledi won with figures like Khaya were a fragile start, not a definitive end. For every parent she convinced, there was a young man whose resentment hardened. The community meetings she held at the heart of the village were attended by many, and her words of empathy and understanding resonated deeply with the girls. But among the young men, a different conversation was brewing, a dangerous undercurrent of anger that she couldn't reach with a simple dialogue. They saw her not as a peacemaker, but as the woman who had stripped them of their traditions and power.

The backlash began subtly, a new kind of battle Naledi had not fully anticipated. Girls who attended her meetings and expressed a desire to continue their education began to find themselves the targets of a quiet, insidious form of harassment. Their names would appear in whispered rumors that spread faster than Naledi's message of hope. Photos, once shared innocently, were now posted online with cruel captions. The old customs had been forced to adapt, and this new generation of resistance was fighting with modern weapons—social media, shame, and gossip.

Zola, whose courage had been the initial spark, was one of the first victims. A photo of her with Naledi, taken at the women's center, was posted in a private group chat of village boys. The caption beneath it was venomous and full of lies, portraying her as disloyal to her family and a traitor to her own people. The shame, once a village-wide rumor, was now a viral sensation in their small, digital world. Zola was a bright, determined girl, but the weight of the online shaming was a heavy burden, and Naledi saw a familiar fear creep into her eyes.

Naledi realized this was not an isolated incident. A young man, a cousin of Sipho's named Bonga, had returned to the village. He was a charismatic leader, and he carried with him a bitterness that had been nurtured from a distance. Sipho, from his prison cell, had been writing to his family, his letters filled with a distorted narrative of his martyrdom. He had not only lost his freedom, he had convinced himself, but he had become a symbol of a man who was punished for honoring his people's ways.

Bonga, a boy who had once idolized his older cousin, now saw himself as a protector of Sipho's honor. He was the one organizing the digital attacks, using modern tools to enforce ancient prejudices. He saw Naledi as the enemy, a personification of the city that had taken everything from his family. He was not a bully; he was a revolutionary, a defender of a past he had never truly known.

Naledi, Thembi, and Jabulani sat in the women's center, staring at a small screen, scrolling through the vile comments. The insults, the lies, the threats—it was a digital poison that was contaminating the very peace they were trying to build. This was a new kind of war, a new kind of pain. They could not simply call the police. They could not simply hold a court. The enemy was invisible, and its weapon was a whisper.

As Naledi looked at the screen, she saw a new comment on a post about Zola. It was from an anonymous account, but the words were a chilling echo of the past. "This is not over," it read. "The city cannot defeat us. We will get our honor back." Naledi felt a cold knot of dread tighten in her stomach. It was a direct threat, a promise of a reckoning to come. She had won the battle in court, but the war, it seemed, was just beginning. She had to find a new way to fight, a way to defeat an enemy who was not just a person, but an idea, a ghost of the past that refused to die.

CHAPTER 25: FIGHTING AN INVISIBLE ENEMY

The chilling message on the screen, "This is not over," was a poison-tipped arrow shot from a ghost. Naledi felt a familiar cold dread, but it was laced with a new kind of frustration. This was not a physical threat that could be addressed with a police raid or a legal summons. This was an idea, a digital poison spreading through the village's social fabric. She could not simply call Ms. Maseko; the law, in this new battlefield, was a blunt instrument.

She, Thembi, and Jabulani sat in the women's center long into the night, the small screen a window into the dark heart of the village's new resistance. Thembi, her face a road map of weary wisdom, shook her head. "They are using the city's tools to fight us," she said. "They are angry, Naledi. They feel that their pride was taken from them, and now they are taking it out on the girls."

Jabulani, who had always been a quiet presence, spoke with a new resolve. "This is not about honor," he said. "This is about cowardice. A man with honor does not hide behind a screen to harm a child."

Naledi looked at the screen again, at the vicious comments and the viral rumors. She knew they couldn't respond with legal threats. That would only fuel Bonga's narrative of martyrdom. She couldn't hold another meeting; that would only make the girls more visible targets. She had to fight fire with fire, to use the same tools of communication against the very people who were using them for malice.

The next day, Naledi gathered the girls at the women's center. She spoke to them not as a lawyer, but as a leader, a survivor who understood their fear. "They are trying to silence you with shame," she said. "But shame only works if you let it. We are not going to fight their lies with our anger. We are going to fight them with our truth."

She laid out her new strategy: a digital counter-campaign. They would not respond to the hateful comments or engage in the rumors. Instead, they would use the very same platforms to tell a different story. The campaign was simple and powerful, an initiative she called "Our Stories, Our Future." Each girl would create a short video, a post, or a photo that told a simple, honest story about her dreams. The girls spoke of wanting to be teachers, nurses, entrepreneurs, and artists. They spoke of their pride in their community and their hope for a future where boys and girls could grow together.

Zola, her initial fear now replaced by a quiet courage, was the first to create a video. She stood in front of her home, her voice clear and strong. "They say I am a traitor for wanting to be a teacher," she said, looking directly at the camera. "But a teacher is not a traitor. A teacher is a leader. I want to teach the children of this village. I want to build a better future for my community." The video was simple, but it was powerful.

The videos and posts began to spread, amplified by Naledi's own network of city friends and media contacts. The campaign was an elegant and devastating response to Bonga's bitterness. The hate-filled comments of his small group were now buried under a mountain of positivity and hope. The village community, which had been so divided, now had a new story to follow—a story of brave, determined young women who were not running away from their home, but fighting for its future.

For the first time, Bonga found himself on the back foot. His attempts at shaming were no longer working. The boys who had once followed him with blind loyalty were now questioning his tactics. He saw his power slipping away, his narrative of righteous indignation crumbling in the face of Naledi's powerful, unified message. He was losing.

In a fit of escalating rage, Bonga, no longer hiding behind anonymous accounts, posted a direct and chilling threat on his own social media page. It was a photo of the women's center, with a single, ominous line of text: "The problem is with the foundation. We will fix it." The digital war had now crossed a new line. It was no longer a battle of words and rumors, but a clear, personal threat of physical violence. Naledi, seeing the post, felt a cold knot of fear tighten in her stomach. The ghost of the past, she realized, had finally come out of the shadows.

CHAPTER 26: THE RECKONING

The chilling photo of the women's center, a beacon of hope and progress, now looked like a target. Bonga's ominous text, "The problem is with the foundation. We will fix it," was a direct and undeniable threat of physical violence. The subtle, digital war of whispers and rumors had just crossed the line into a dangerous, tangible reality. Naledi, Thembi, and Jabulani, staring at the small screen, felt a cold knot of dread tighten in their stomachs. This was no longer a battle of ideas; it was a fight for their safety.

The digital counter-campaign that had been so effective now seemed like a fragile shield. Naledi knew she couldn't respond with another video. This was a direct threat against the physical structure that represented everything they had fought for, and against the girls who found sanctuary there. She looked at Thembi and Jabulani, their faces a mixture of fear and determination. "It's time to call the police," Naledi said, her voice quiet and firm. This was a job for the law, not a social media campaign.

She made the call, her hands shaking slightly as she spoke to the dispatcher. She explained the situation, the history of resentment, and the escalating digital harassment that had culminated in this final, chilling threat. The police, hearing the details, promised to send an officer to the village immediately. Naledi felt a small sense of relief, but she knew that they couldn't simply wait for the law to arrive. Bonga had been pushed to a dangerous edge, and his escalating rage was a fire that could no longer be contained by reason.

They immediately began to mobilize the community. Thembi, with a quiet strength that had been honed by years of struggle, began calling the mothers of the girls who frequented the center. They needed to ensure the girls were safe and that no one was left alone. Jabulani, for his part, went to a small group of village men who had quietly supported their cause from the beginning, men who believed in a new future for their community. He explained the threat, not with fear, but with a call to action.

The men, a small but resolute group, gathered near the women's center. They were not warriors, but fathers and husbands, men who had seen the old ways lead to pain and who had chosen a new, more difficult path. They sat vigil, their quiet presence a silent, powerful promise of protection. They were not just guarding a building; they were guarding an idea, a future for their daughters and a new kind of honor for their community.

As night fell, a small group of young men, led by a charismatic and furious Bonga, began to gather on the outskirts of the village. Their phones were lit up with messages of bravado and rage, their anger fueled by a distorted narrative of injustice and a profound sense of humiliation. Bonga, in his mind, was not a criminal; he was a liberator, a hero who was about to restore the honor that had been taken from his family.

He had expected the village to be a sea of fearful, silent people. He had expected to find a community that was too afraid to stand up to his threats. But as he and his followers began to approach the women's center, they saw a group of men sitting outside, their faces grim and determined. And then, he saw Naledi. She was standing in front of the center, a woman who was no longer just a ghost from the past, but a resolute leader of a new future. Bonga had expected a battle, but he had found a reckoning.

CHAPTER 27: THE RECKONINGS END

The flickering light of a single bulb from the women's center cast long, dancing shadows across the yard, illuminating the grim faces of the men who stood in vigil. The silence was absolute, broken only by the sound of approaching footsteps and the low murmur of young men's voices. Bonga, his face contorted with fury, emerged from the darkness, his followers at his back, their phones clutched in their hands like modern-day weapons. He had expected to find a deserted building, a symbol of the city's meddling that he could destroy. Instead, he found a wall of silent, resolute men and, standing in front of them, Naledi.

Bonga stopped dead in his tracks, his eyes wide with surprise and rage. He had prepared for a battle against a building, not a confrontation with people. "What is this?" he shouted, his voice cracking with a mixture of bravado and shock. He looked at the men, men he had known his whole life, men who were now standing with the enemy. "You are traitors! You stand with her, the woman who took our honor from us?"

Naledi stepped forward, her body small and seemingly fragile, but her voice was a steel wire, taut with authority. "No one took your honor, Bonga," she said, her voice clear and unwavering in the night. "You are giving it away, every time you hide behind a screen to threaten a child. You are giving it away, every time you choose to shame a young woman instead of supporting her. This center is not the enemy. The women here are not the enemy. The only enemy here is the anger that blinds you to the truth."

Her words hit him like a physical blow. He lunged forward, his face a mask of pure hatred. "You think you are so clever?" he screamed. "You think you have all the answers? You ruined my family! You took my cousin, and now you are taking everything else!"

But before he could reach her, two of the men stepped forward, placing a hand on his chest. It was Jabulani, and with him, Khaya, the very man Naledi had convinced to support his daughter's dreams. "This is enough, Bonga," Jabulani said, his voice low and firm. "You may have lost your way, but we have not. This place is not a problem. It is a promise. It is the promise of a better future for our children."

The moment hung in the air, a tense and fragile stalemate. The boys with Bonga, seeing the unified front of the village men, began to falter. They had been prepared to fight a ghost, an idea. They had not been prepared to stand against their fathers, their uncles, and their neighbors. Bonga looked at his followers, seeing their doubt, and for the first time, he felt his power slipping away.

Just then, the wail of sirens broke the night's stillness. The police van, its lights flashing, turned into the village, a jarring, official presence that broke the spell of the confrontation. The officers, led by a calm and focused Sergeant, stepped out, their faces grim. Bonga's bravado completely evaporated. He saw the law, not as an abstract idea, but as a real and present force. He was no longer a martyr. He was a criminal.

The officers arrested Bonga, and as they led him away, he shouted one last, venomous threat at Naledi. "This is not over!" But the shout was a hollow one, a final, pathetic echo of his cousin's rage. The boys who had followed him, their heads bowed in shame, were simply told to go home. The reckoning was over. The night was quiet once again.

Naledi, Thembi, and Jabulani stood together, watching the police lights fade into the distance. The vigil was over, but the victory was a profound one. It was not just a legal victory; it was a community victory. The men who had stood with Naledi were no longer just passive observers; they were active participants in a new kind of future. Naledi's legal fight had brought justice, but her quiet, persistent advocacy had brought something far more powerful: a new kind of peace, a peace built not on fear, but on the quiet, resolute strength of a community united. The journey, she knew, was a long one. But tonight, for the first time, she truly believed that the new dawn was here to stay.

CHAPTER 28: THE NEW FOUNDATION

The police van's red and blue lights faded into the distance, taking with them Bonga and his misplaced rage. The night was quiet once more, but it was a different kind of quiet—a silence filled not with fear, but with a profound, shared purpose. The men who had stood vigil slowly dispersed, their heads held high. They had not fought with fists or spears; they had stood firm, a silent, unyielding wall against the old, broken ways. They had chosen to protect an idea, and in doing so, they had given their community a new kind of honor.

Naledi, Thembi, and Jabulani remained for a long while, standing in the middle of the yard. The women's center, a beacon of hope just moments before, now felt like a living monument to their collective courage. Jabulani looked at Naledi, his eyes filled with a deep, quiet respect. "You did not come with the law this time," he said, his voice soft. "You came with an idea. And the idea was stronger than the anger."

Naledi nodded, a wave of profound peace washing over her. She realized that her journey had been a full circle. She had fought to be free from her community, and now, she was fighting to make her community free from itself. The legal victories, the public statements—they had all been necessary. But the true change had begun tonight, on this very ground, when the men of the village had chosen to stand with their daughters, with their future.

The following morning, Naledi and Thembi held a meeting at the women's center, but this time, it was not just for the girls. The young men who had followed Bonga, their faces filled with a mixture of shame and confusion, were there as well. Naledi spoke to them not as a lawyer or an enemy, but as a person who understood their pain. She spoke of Sipho's rage, of his life ruined by a lie, and of Bonga's attempt to repeat the same tragic cycle. She did not condemn them; she offered them a new path.

"Your anger is not the problem," she said, her voice gentle. "The problem is where you put it. You can put it into shaming girls online, and you will end up where Bonga and Sipho are. Or, you can put it into building something better. You can become the protectors of a new kind of honor, a new kind of pride." She spoke of her own struggle, of the power of a family that supports its children's dreams, and of a community that rises together.

The conversation that followed was long and difficult, but it was filled with a new kind of honesty. The boys, who had been so quick to anger, began to speak of their own fears—of being forgotten by the city, of losing their traditions, of a world that seemed to be leaving them behind. Naledi listened, and for the first time, she truly saw them not as enemies, but as children, caught in the same struggle as she had been, a long time ago.

As the sun began to set, Naledi stood on the koppie, looking at the village below. The women's center, a small white building, was a silent testament to her journey. She had come here as a child, lost in a world she didn't understand. She had left as a victim, a symbol of a cultural war. She had returned as a woman, a lawyer, a leader, and a voice for a new generation. Her journey had not been about escaping the past; it had been about transforming it.

The war was not over. The road to true peace would be long and difficult, a continuous process of dialogue, education, and healing. But as she looked at the village, at the men who had stood in vigil, at the boys who were now listening, at the girls who were dreaming of a new future, she knew that the battle had been won. The old foundation had crumbled, and a new one, built on the quiet, resolute strength of a community united, was finally taking shape.

CHAPTER 29: THE HARVEST OF COURAGE

The embers of conflict had cooled, and from the ashes, a new, more resilient community was forged. The foundation of the women's center, once a symbol of division, was now the heart of a united village. The young men who had once followed Bonga's path of resentment now found a new kind of purpose. Inspired by Naledi's message, they began to use their digital skills not for shame, but for empowerment, creating a community website that celebrated the village's traditions while also highlighting the achievements of its young people, particularly the girls.

Naledi, over the next few years, became a pivotal figure in a national movement. Her law firm, in partnership with the women's center, launched a legal education program that was implemented in rural communities across the country. She trained a new generation of lawyers and activists, young women who, like her, had experienced the painful intersection of tradition and law. The precedent set by her case was now a powerful tool, a beacon of justice for countless others. Her journey had not been a solo fight, but a catalyst for a national change.

One quiet afternoon, Naledi received an unexpected letter. It was from the prison, a short, formal note informing her of Sipho's upcoming release. He had served his sentence, a long and lonely time in which his rage had slowly, but irrevocably, turned to a profound and empty silence. When he returned to the village, he was not a martyr or a hero. He was a broken man. He lived a life of quiet solitude, a ghost in a community that had moved on without him. The boy who had tried to steal a future had lost his own, a tragic and bitter end to a story that should have been a celebration.

Mkhulu, for his part, never fully recovered from the shame and defeat of the trial. His authority had been irreparably damaged, his pride shattered. He lived out his final years as a man of quiet contemplation, a living monument to a world that was slowly, but surely, fading away. In his final days, he saw the young girls of the village—confident, educated, and free—and perhaps in that, he saw not a betrayal of his legacy, but a new, more powerful kind of honor. His death, when it came, was a quiet and peaceful one, a final farewell to a world that was no longer his.

The true legacy of Naledi's fight was not a court case or a legal precedent. It was a harvest of courage. It was Thembi, now an elder herself, using her newfound authority to mentor young girls, her quiet strength a guiding light. It was Jabulani, the quietest of men, who became a powerful voice for change, a symbol of a man who had the courage to choose a new path. And it was Zola, who, years later, returned to the village as a teacher, her classroom a place of laughter and learning, a living testament to the power of a single girl's dream.

Naledi's final trip to the village was not for a case or a meeting. It was for a celebration. A new women's center, a permanent structure built of brick and stone, was being opened. As she stood on the stage, looking at the faces of her friends, her family, and the young girls who were now looking at her not as a symbol, but as a sister, she felt a profound sense of peace. Her journey had not been about escaping the village, but about bringing a new dawn to it. The trauma was a part of her story, but it was not her destiny. Her destiny, she realized, was here, in this place, with these people, at the heart of a community that had found its soul again.

CHAPTER 30: A NEW CASE, A LASTING LEGACY

The new women's center, a testament to a community's resilience, was now the backdrop for Naledi's new life. It was a place where she felt the deep, quiet rhythm of a world she had helped to build. The harvest of courage, as she had once called it, was now a thriving, vibrant crop. Her journey had not ended with a verdict; it had blossomed into a mission.

One afternoon, a small, quiet girl named Thandi was brought to her by Zola, who was now a confident, respected teacher and a key community organizer for the center. Thandi's face was filled with a familiar fear, a silent terror that Naledi knew all too well. Thandi's story was an echo of Naledi's own, but it was also a painful testament to how the old ways had evolved into a new kind of cruelty. Thandi had not been abducted. She had been promised a scholarship to a city school, a promise made by a charismatic older boy who had used her dreams against her. He had then demanded a 'bride price' from her family, threatening to expose a private correspondence between them if she did not comply. He had used her own ambitions as a weapon, and the city's promise of education as a lure for his own gain.

The case was a new kind of challenge. There was no physical force, no public abduction. The crime was a subtle form of coercion, a digital manipulation that was harder to prove, a crime that existed in the gray areas between tradition and a new, more insidious kind of emotional blackmail. Naledi listened to Thandi's story, her heart heavy, but a new resolve burning in her eyes. The legal fight had changed, and she had to change with it.

She worked with Zola, who, with her deep understanding of the new digital landscape, began to gather evidence from the community. They spoke to other girls who had been victims of the same subtle pressure. They built a case not on physical evidence, but on a pattern of emotional and psychological manipulation. They were not fighting a custom; they were fighting a crime that was using a custom as a shield. The old laws were not enough. They needed a new, more creative legal strategy.

Naledi, now a respected lawyer with a national reputation, found her new purpose not in the grand halls of justice, but in the quiet, dignified rooms of the women's center. She worked with Thembi, a new kind of elder who offered not just quiet wisdom but a fierce, protective love for the girls in her community. And she worked with Jabulani, the quietest of men, who had become a powerful voice for a new kind of morality, using his influence to gather support from the young men of the village who had learned to choose a new path.

The new case, which came to be known as 'The Thandi Case,' became a landmark. Naledi argued not for a simple criminal charge, but for an injunction against the young man, a legal precedent that would protect girls from emotional and digital blackmail. The case was a long and difficult one, a fight that spanned months. But in the end, Naledi and her team won. The verdict was a clear and unequivocal message: the new kind of cruelty, the digital manipulation, was also a crime. The law, with Naledi's guidance, had adapted to the new times.

In the end, Naledi's legacy was not just a legal one. It was a human one. It was Zola, standing at the front of a classroom, a young woman who was not just a teacher but a beacon of hope for a new generation. It was Thembi, an elder who had the courage to choose a new path for her people. And it was Thandi, a girl who, with Naledi's help, went to a new school, her dreams of education not stolen, but protected. Naledi's journey had not ended with a verdict. It had begun a new dawn, a new, more lasting legacy of courage and hope, a legacy that would continue to grow, one girl, one dream, one quiet victory at a time.

CHAPTER 31: A SEAT A THE TABLE

The legal victory in 'The Thandi Case' was a watershed moment. It sent a clear message that the law could adapt to protect young women from new, more subtle forms of coercion. The injunction Naledi secured became a powerful precedent, a legal shield that was now being used in courts across the nation. The women's center in the village, once a local safe haven, was now a model for similar organizations, and Naledi's name became synonymous with a new kind of justice—one that honored tradition without sacrificing the rights of the individual.

Naledi's legal reputation soared. She was no longer just the young lawyer who had won a landmark case. She was a national figure, a powerful voice for a generation of women caught between two worlds. Her work was celebrated in the media, and she was invited to speak at universities and legal conferences, her story of courage and resilience a powerful testament to the change she had helped to bring about.

This newfound prominence led to an unexpected offer. The President's office, under increasing pressure to address the complex issues of traditional law and women's rights, announced the formation of a national commission. They needed a chair, a leader who could navigate the delicate balance between progress and tradition, a voice that could speak to both worlds. The offer, to Naledi's shock and surprise, was extended to her.

She discussed the offer with her parents, Thembi, and Jabulani. Her father, Thabo, his face filled with a quiet pride, was the first to speak. "This is it, Naledi," he said, his voice soft. "This is what all of this was for. You didn't just win a battle. You won a seat at the table. You are no longer just fighting. You are now helping to write the rules."

But Thembi, with her deep, earthy wisdom, was more cautious. "A seat at the table," she said, her voice a low murmur, "is a place where you will be surrounded by people who do not want you there. They will smile at you, but they will be waiting for you to fall. They will not see you as Naledi. They will see you as a symbol, an enemy of their way of life."

The reality of Thembi's words was not lost on Naledi. This was a new kind of battlefield, a political one, where the weapons were not legal arguments but public opinion and power. She knew that her success would not be celebrated by everyone. She had already seen the subtle animosity in the press from a powerful political figure, a minister named Mr. Khumalo, a man with a long history of public support for traditional leadership and a known critic of her past work. He had painted her as a radical, an agent of the city who was trying to destroy the very fabric of their culture. He was a powerful and dangerous enemy, a man who saw her not just as a lawyer, but as a political threat.

Naledi accepted the offer. She was a different person now. She was not the scared child who had been taken. She was not the lawyer who had fought for her own justice. She was a leader, a voice, and a symbol of a new kind of future. She knew the road ahead would be difficult, filled with political landmines and powerful enemies. But she also knew that the battle for justice, for a new kind of peace, was not fought in the courtroom. It was fought in the hearts and minds of a nation. And she was now at the heart of it, with a seat at the table, ready for the next fight.

CHAPTER 32: THE POLITICAL ARENA

The commission's office was a world away from the dusty earth of the village and the tense atmosphere of the courtroom. Housed in a pristine government building, the room was all polished wood, leather chairs, and hushed tones. Naledi felt the weight of the air, thick with the scent of ambition and power. She sat at the head of a long mahogany table, her new title—Chairperson—feeling both a profound honor and a heavy burden. The battle for justice had left the personal realm and entered the political, and the rules of engagement were entirely different.

The commission members filed in, a cross-section of the nation's complexities. There was a stoic, silver-haired traditional chief, a woman academic from a prestigious university, a young, eager human rights lawyer, and a few seasoned politicians. Each of them represented a different world, a different set of beliefs, and a different vision for the nation's future. Naledi knew her job was not to simply lead them, but to unite them, a task that felt like trying to hold water in her hands.

Just as the meeting was about to begin, the door swung open, and Mr. Khumalo made his entrance. He was a large man with an imposing presence, a practiced politician's smile that didn't quite reach his eyes. He walked to his seat, a subtle power in his stride, a quiet assertion that this room, and this commission, was his domain. He did not look at Naledi. He looked at the other members, a silent message passing between them. He was not a member of the commission, but he was a powerful minister, and his presence was a clear warning.

The meeting began with Naledi's opening remarks. She spoke not of the law, but of a shared future, of a nation that could honor its past without sacrificing the rights of its children. She spoke with a quiet passion, her voice calm and resolute. When she finished, a quiet, respectful silence filled the room. But it was broken by Mr. Khumalo, who, without a word, pushed his chair back and stood up, a clear signal that he was about to speak.

"A beautiful sentiment, Chairperson," he said, his voice dripping with condescension. "A beautiful, idealistic sentiment. But what is the practical reality? The people I represent, the people of the villages, do not want to be saved. They want to be heard. They want to be respected. They want their traditions, their very way of life, to be protected from... well, from people who do not understand them." He did not look at Naledi. He looked at the traditional chief, a silent challenge in his gaze.

The attack was subtle and well-timed, a direct hit to the very heart of Naledi's legitimacy. He was painting her as an outsider, a city girl with no understanding of the real world. A sudden, cold anger rose in Naledi's chest, but she suppressed it. This was not a courtroom. She could not respond with a legal argument. She had to respond with political cunning.

She looked at Mr. Khumalo, and a small, knowing smile played on her lips. "I understand your concern, Minister," she said, her voice still calm and professional. "Which is precisely why I believe this commission is so important. It is about understanding, not about saving. It is about listening, not about telling. I am a child of the village. I know what it is to be a child of this land. My job is not to save them. My job is to ensure that every voice, from the most powerful chief to the most vulnerable girl, is heard. I would assume, Minister, that is a mission we can both agree on."

The retort, so elegant and disarming, hung in the air. She had used his own words against him, turning his subtle attack into a shared mission. His smile faltered for a moment, the mask of a seasoned politician slipping just enough for her to see the pure, unadulterated hatred that lay beneath. He simply nodded, a silent acknowledgment of the new game they were playing, and left the room.

Naledi looked at the commission members, her eyes meeting theirs. The battle had begun, and the stakes were higher than ever. The fight was no longer for her own justice. It was for the soul of a nation. And she was now at the heart of it, with a seat at the table, ready for the long, political war ahead.

CHAPTER 33: THE FIRST GAMBIT

The silence that followed Mr. Khumalo's exit was heavy and charged. The commission members, who had been an assortment of individuals moments before, were now a single, unified audience, their eyes fixed on Naledi. She had just faced down a political heavyweight in his own territory, and their collective reaction was one of cautious appraisal. The stoic traditional chief, his face a road map of quiet wisdom, gave a single, almost imperceptible nod. It was a silent acknowledgment of her cunning and resilience, a sign that she had passed his first test.

Naledi did not gloat or get angry. She simply took a slow, calming breath and brought the meeting back to order. "Thank you, everyone," she said, her voice steady and professional. "Now that we have dispensed with the theatrics, perhaps we can begin the work of building a new framework for our nation's future." Her calm demeanor and sharp wit disarmed the room, and the meeting proceeded with a renewed sense of purpose.

The internal battles were just as fierce as the external ones. The human rights lawyer, an idealistic young woman named Zandile, was eager to push for radical, swift change. The traditional chief, a man named Chief Mkhize, insisted on a slower, more deliberate pace, arguing for the preservation of ancestral customs. The academic, a brilliant but cautious woman named Dr. Ndlovu, wanted to ground every decision in data and research. And the politicians, ever-aware of public opinion, sought a middle ground that would appease everyone without making any meaningful concessions.

Naledi found herself caught in the middle, a mediator in a war of ideologies. She spent hours listening to each of them, her own experiences a powerful anchor. She spoke with Chief Mkhize, not as a lawyer, but as a child of the village, sharing stories of her own family and her own community. She spoke with Zandile, not as a superior, but as a colleague, reminding her that progress, to be lasting, had to be built on the foundation of understanding, not force. She had learned a long time ago that you could not simply dismantle an idea; you had to replace it with a better one.

But the political arena was a battle on two fronts. While Naledi was working to build consensus from within, Mr. Khumalo was working to dismantle her from the outside. The next day, the news was filled with articles and talk show segments painting Naledi as an elitist, a city girl who had forgotten her roots. The stories twisted her words, portraying her as an enemy of tradition who was using her personal story to push a radical, anti-cultural agenda. The attack was swift, venomous, and dangerously effective.

Her phone rang, a familiar number from the village. It was Thembi. "We see what they are doing, child," Thembi said, her voice a low, comforting murmur. "He is trying to make you angry. He wants you to lose your heart. He wants you to forget where you come from. But you must not. Remember that a tree with deep roots can withstand any storm."

The wisdom of the words was a balm to Naledi's weary spirit. She realized that her political battle was not just about the law or policy. It was about narrative. Khumalo was trying to tell a story of an outsider who had come to destroy a culture. Her job, she realized, was to tell a different story, a story of a child of the village who had come to build a new and better future. She was no longer just the chairperson of a commission; she was the storyteller of a nation. The long, political war had just begun, and Naledi, with her roots firmly planted in the earth of her home, was ready to fight.

DEDICATION

To the women and girls who, with quiet courage, stand as baobab trees in the wind.

This book is for you—for those who found their voice in the face of silence, and for the communities who chose to build a new dawn. Your stories are the true foundation of justice, and your strength is the harvest that will forever nourish the land.

For Thembi and Jabulani, for Thabo and Lerato, and for every parent who chose to believe in their child's dream.

ABOUT AN AUTHOR

Sibongiseni Masengemu is a celebrated South African writer who, through his work, serves as a passionate voice for his society and culture. His writing is dedicated to exploring the complex intersection of culture, life, and the law.

Born and raised in a rural community, Masengemu draws deeply from his personal experiences and a profound understanding of his heritage. He has a profound passion for writing about law and culture, and this book represents his first foray into writing about the legal challenges faced by marginalized communities. His writing is known for its empathetic approach and its success in bridging the gap between traditional practices and modern legal frameworks.

UKUTHWALA BRIDE is his debut novel, a powerful and poignant story that serves as an educational reference for university students. Through his writing, Masengemu seeks not only to entertain but to educate society and serve as a voice for the voiceless, continuing the crucial conversation about cultural evolution, justice, and the unwavering strength of the human spirit. He continues to be an influential figure in the national dialogue on human rights.

CLOSING GLOSSARY

Key Terms and Characters

- **Bonga:** Sipho's cousin, a young man who uses social media to lead a new, subtle form of harassment against the village girls, fueled by bitterness and a misguided sense of loyalty to Sipho.
- **Chief Mkhize:** The traditional chief who sits on the national commission. He represents the voice of ancestral customs and initially views Naledi with cautious appraisal, but eventually shows her a measure of respect.
- **Jabulani:** Thembi's husband and Naledi's uncle. A quiet and thoughtful man who chooses to stand with his family and new ideals, becoming a powerful voice for change in the village.
- **Koppie:** A small hill or rise. It is the location where Naledi was initially taken by Sipho and his friends. It later becomes a place of reflection and hope for Naledi.
- **Lerato:** Naledi's mother. She is a woman of quiet, steadfast strength who provides unwavering emotional support to her daughter throughout her ordeal.
- **Mr. Khumalo:** A powerful minister and political rival of Naledi. He is a staunch supporter of traditional leadership and uses his influence to publicly discredit and undermine Naledi's work on the commission.
- **Mkhulu:** Sipho's grandfather and a powerful village elder. He is a staunch defender of the old ways and is arrested for his role in Naledi's kidnapping. He eventually dies a defeated man, unable to reconcile with a changing world.
- **Ms. Maseko:** Naledi's sharp and pragmatic lawyer. She guides Naledi through the trial, acting as both a legal advocate and a mentor, and is a key figure in Naledi's legal success.
- **Naledi:** The story's protagonist. A young woman who is

kidnapped under the custom of *ukuthwala*. She finds the courage to speak her truth, becomes a lawyer, and eventually rises to national prominence, fighting for women's rights and a modern interpretation of justice.

- **Sipho:** Naledi's cousin who, under the custom of *ukuthwala*, tries to kidnap her for marriage. He is arrested and sentenced to prison, where he remains filled with bitterness, convinced he was a martyr to a lost cause.
- **Thabo:** Naledi's father. A man who left the village for a new life in the city, he fights tirelessly for his daughter's freedom and justice, providing a quiet but powerful force of support.
- **Thembi:** Naledi's aunt and a resident of the village. She is a compassionate woman who helps Naledi and her family and becomes an early advocate for change in her community, despite the social cost.
- **The women's center:** A safe haven and resource hub in the village that Naledi and her allies help to establish. It provides education, legal support, and a community for girls, eventually becoming a national model.
- ***Ukuthwala:*** A traditional custom in the village, initially described as a forced marriage by abduction. Through Naledi's journey, it is reformed to be a practice that requires the consent and safety of the young woman.
- **Zola:** A young girl in the village who is inspired by Naledi's advocacy. She becomes an early target of digital harassment but bravely chooses to speak out, later becoming a teacher and a key leader at the women's center.

BOOK GENRE

Based on the story's narrative, the genre is a **Legal and Political Drama**.

It also contains strong elements of:

- **Coming-of-Age:** We follow the main character, Naledi, from her youth to her adulthood as she finds her purpose.
- **Social Commentary:** The story explores the conflict between traditional customs and modern laws, focusing on themes of women's rights and community change.

Don't miss out!

Visit the website below and you can sign up to receive emails whenever Sibongiseni Masengemu publishes a new book. There's no charge and no obligation.

https://books2read.com/r/B-A-LADUC-GFITG

BOOKS 2 READ

Connecting independent readers to independent writers.

www.ingramcontent.com/pod-product-compliance
Lightning Source LLC
LaVergne TN
LVHW022112200926
848481LV00003B/1153
* 9 7 9 8 2 3 1 5 9 0 8 8 9 *